Illustrated Korean Traditional Cooking

Korean Mother's Easy Recipes

Illustrated Korean Traditional Cooking

Korean Mother's Easy Recipes

Recipes and Cooking Yoon Okhee
Illustrations Chae Jinjoo

Carlsbad, CA and Seoul

Illustrated Korean Traditional Cooking
Korean Mother's Easy Recipes

Copyright © 2019 by Yoon Okhee, Chae Jinjoo

Translated & proofread by Chung Dayoung, Alex Sigrist
Edited by Hahm Minji
Designed by Lee Hyehee, Oh JiHye

All rights reserved. No part of this publication may be reproduced or utilized in any form or by any means, electronic or mechanical, including photocopying, recording, or by any information storage and retrieval system, without prior written permission from the copyright holders.

First published in 2019
Sixth printing, 2024
by Hollym International Corp., Carlsbad, CA, USA
Phone 760 814 9880
www.hollym.com   **e-Mail** contact@hollym.com

 Hollym

Published simultaneously in Korea
by Hollym Corp., Publishers, Seoul, Korea
Phone +82 2 734 5087   **Fax** +82 2 730 5149
www.hollym.net   **e-Mail** hollym@hollym.co.kr

ISBN: 978-1-56591-494-0
Library of Congress Control Number: 2019949420

Printed in Korea

 **A Word from the Author**

What do you say to someone who you want to be friends with? Koreans usually say, "Let's have lunch together sometime!" Having a meal with someone is the same as sharing time with that person and building a relationship.

After teaching Korean cooking to foreigners for 20 years from my cooking school and K-Cooking classes with government institutes, I learned that we can easily understand and communicate with each other through food even though our nationalities, cultures, and languages are different. I also realized that using illustrations would be a fun and effective way of explaining the recipes.

With my diverse experiences I have accumulated as a culinary professional for 40 years, I have written this cookbook hoping that it would be a way of sharing a meal together with anyone who is interested in Korean cuisine. Moreover, I wanted to share my knowledge of traditional Korean cuisine with my daughter, who has illustrated this book; my grandson, who wants to become a chef when he grows up; and my granddaughter, who dreams of opening her own rice cake shop someday.

Based on my own experiences, I have selected dishes popular to foreigners and introduced them with easy-to-understand illustrations and recipes. Aside from a few dishes for special occasions, the recipes will be easy to follow even for beginners to Korean cooking. I hope the readers will experience the authentic taste and flair of Korean cuisine and enjoy the unique culinary culture of Korea.

Lastly, I would like to thank all the people who helped in running the Korean cooking classes, and also the staff of Hollym, who made this publication possible.

Yoon Okhee

About the Author

Recipes and Cooking

Mother Yoon Okhee

Researcher of Korean Cuisine
Master Craftsman Cook and Doctor of Science

Yoon Okhee majored in food and nutrition and went on to lecture at the university level.

She lived in Japan for 4 years where she became interested in food from different parts of the world. Returning to Korea, she learned Korean traditional cuisine from Professor Kang Inhee, a master of Joseon period cuisine, and grew her knowledge and passion for Korean cuisine after studying a Korean traditional medical book, *Donguibogam*.

In addition to more than 20 years of operating her own cooking academy and lecturing at universities, Yoon has expanded her expertise through the Korean family restaurant Sannae Deulnae, the Korea Food and Culture Institute, and the Cheong Wa Dae Sarangchae Korean Food Experience Center. She now hopes to share the true taste and value of Korean cuisine to her daughter and all those who are interested in Korean cuisine.

Korea Food and Culture Institute Blog
blog.naver.com/yok1425

Instagram
한국요리와 문화 연구소 (@koreafoodandculture_institute)

Other members of the family who appear in this book

Husband
He is happy to eat any food cooked by his wife.

Grandson
He is a connoisseur of delicious food. He wants to become a chef when he grows up.

Granddaughter
Her favorite food is rice cakes. She hopes to become an owner of a rice cake shop.

Illustrations

Daughter Chae Jinjoo

Illustrator & Doll Artist

After studying visual design, she began working as an illustrator and doll artist.

Ever since she was young, Chae has always been interested in drawing, crafts, and the colorful dishes her mother made for her. But her passion was more focused on eating the food rather than the cooking itself. Her interest in cooking grew as she became a mother who tries to regularly make healthy and delicious meals for her children.

She is now ready to learn the taste and value of Korean cuisine from her mother.

Instagram 보들 bodle (@bodlebodle)

You can find the photographs of the dishes on our Instagram "@korean_mothers_easy_recipes." You can also find the Korean version of this book "엄마가 만들고 딸이 그린 한식 레시피."

Son-in-Law

He enjoys cooking. His specialty is *tteokbokki*.

Contents

A Word from the Author • 5
About the Author • 6

Understanding Korean Cuisine • 10
Ingredients for Korean Cuisine • 13
Condiments for Korean Cuisine • 14
Garnishes for Korean Cuisine • 18
Basic Cooking Techniques for Korean Cuisine • 19

Measurements used for this cookbook • 23

Chapter 1

Main Dish

Bap (Rice) • 26
Ogokbap (Steamed Five-grain Rice) • 30
Bibimbap • 34
Gimbap • 38
Hobakjuk · Jatjuk (Pumpkin Porridge · Pine Nut Porridge) • 42
Guksu-jangguk (Noodles in Hot Beef-based Broth) • 46
Mul-naengmyeon (Cold Buckwheat Noodles) • 50
Mandut-guk (Dumpling Soup) • 54

Chapter 2

Side Dish - Guk

Sogogimut-guk (Beef and Radish Soup) • 60
Miyeok-guk (Seaweed Soup) • 64
Sigeumchi Doenjang-guk (Spinach Soybean Paste Soup) • 68

Side Dish - Banchan

Kimchi-jjigae (Kimchi Stew) • 74
Sundubu-jjigae (Soft Bean Curd Stew) • 78
Neobiani (Marinated Grilled Beef Slices) • 82

Dubugui (Pan-fried Bean Curd) • 86
Galbi-jjim (Braised Short Ribs) • 90
Maeun Dak-jjim (Spicy Braised Chicken) • 94
Godeungeo-jorim (Braised Mackerel) • 98
Kimchi-jeon (Kimchi Pancake) • 102
Modum-jeon (Assorted Savory Pancakes) • 106
Bindaetteok (Mung Bean Pancake) • 110
Haemul-pajeon (Seafood and Green Onion Pancake) • 114
Tteokbokki (Spicy Stir-fried Rice Cakes) • 118
Jeyuk-bokkeum (Spicy Stir-fried Pork) • 122
Ttukbaegi-bulgogi (Hot Pot Bulgogi) • 126
Oi-kimchi (Cucumber Kimchi) • 130
Baechu-kimchi (Kimchi) • 134
Kkakdugi (Diced Radish Kimchi) • 138
Nabak-kimchi (Spicy Water Kimchi) • 142
Samsaek-namul (Three Seasoned Vegetables) • 146

Chapter 3

Special Dish

Sinseollo (Royal Hot Pot) • 152
Gujeolpan (Platter of Nine Delicacies) • 158
Japchae (Stir-fried Glass Noodles and Vegetables) • 164
Gungjung-tteokbokki (Royal Stir-fried Rice Cakes) • 168
Samgyetang (Ginseng Chicken Soup) • 172
Bossam (Napa Wraps with Pork) • 176

Chapter 4

Dessert & Drink

Baekseolgi (Snow White Rice Cake) • 182
Hwajeon (Pan-fried Flower Rice Cake) • 186
Omija-hwachae (Omija Punch) • 190
Sujeonggwa (Cinnamon Punch) • 194

Index • 198

Understanding Korean Cuisine

A wide variety of ingredients are used for cooking.
Koreans use vegetables and meat products in a ratio of 8:2.

Various fermented foods are used for cooking.
Different kinds of fermented foods including *ganjang* (soy sauce), *doenjang* (soybean paste), *gochujang* (red chili paste), and salted seafood, are used as condiments to season the dishes. Among these items, soy sauce is used as the base seasoning. Fermented dishes, such as kimchi and pickles, are also made.

Koreans enjoy seasonal food.
Koreans enjoy a traditional culinary culture of making dishes with fresh seasonal ingredients. These nutritious dishes, made with different ingredients from each season, and the traditional holiday dishes create a distinctive Korean culinary culture.

The Korean table is set in *"Bansangcharim"* form.

Bansangcharim is a form of Korean table setting with rice as the main dish served with soup and various side dishes. The side dishes, made with different seasonal ingredients of vegetables, meat, fish, and marine plants, are nutritionally well-balanced and rich in color.

A Korean traditional table setting can be called 3 (*sam*)-*cheop*, 5 (*o*)-*cheop*, 7 (*chil*)-*cheop* or 9 (*gu*)-*cheop* depending on the number of side dishes—not including the basic dishes of rice, *guk* (soup), *jjigae* (stew), kimchi, and *jang* (fermented condiment). 12 (*sipyi*)-*cheop* was made exclusively in the royal court.

In the past, diners had their own individual small setting of food, but nowadays, this has changed to having individual bowls of rice and soup and sharing the side dishes together. On special occasions, many different kinds of dishes would be made for the meal, but usually Koreans eat rice, soup or stew, and kimchi as their basic meal and add several side dishes to it.

Example of 3-*cheop* Table
Extra side dishes: *namul* (seasoned vegetables), braised fish, toasted laver

Example of Today's Table

Example of 7-*cheop* Table
Extra side dishes: seasoned radish, assorted *namul* (seasoned vegetables), grilled dried pollack, braised beef, savory pancakes, stir-fried chilis and anchovies, pan-fried cucumber pickles

Korean cuisine is a food of "*Yaksikdongwon*."

In Korean culture and those of other Asian countries, there is an ancient philosophy of *Yin-Yang* Five Elements. This is the belief that the world was created by two opposing energies of yin and yang, and the form of five elements—water, tree, fire, earth, and metal.

For a long time, Koreans saw the human body as a small universe, balanced by the *Yin-Yang* Five Elements, and thought that food should be consumed under this belief to maintain good health and to prevent and cure illnesses. Each dish is nutritionally well-balanced and carefully made with a balance of flavor and various other traits and garnished with different ingredients representing one (or more) of the five colors. Korean traditional cuisine is a food of *Yaksikdongwon*, an idea that food can prevent and cure illness as medicine and food arise from the same source.

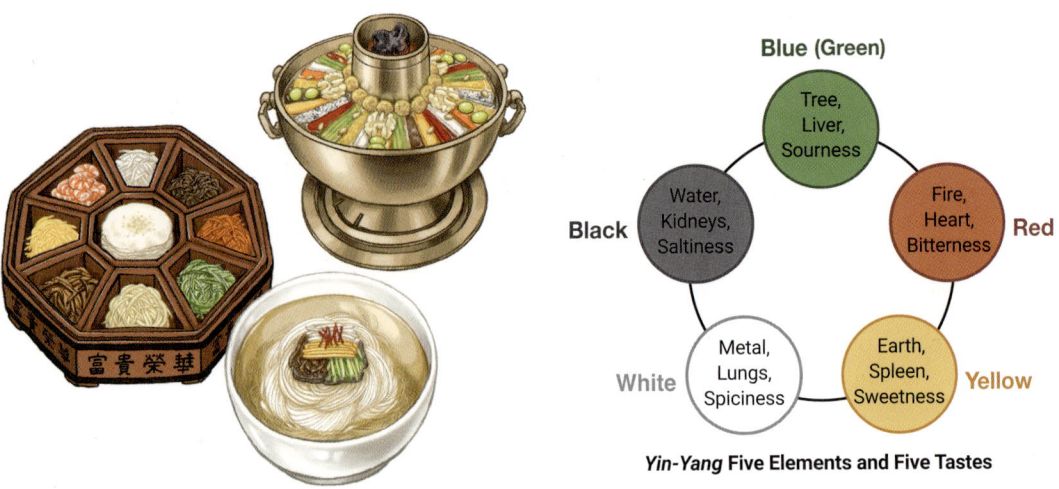

Yin-Yang Five Elements and Five Tastes

Donguibogam, a Korean traditional medical book

Donguibogam was written by a royal physician Heo Jun (1539–1615), in 1610 on orders from King Seonjo. It focuses on the different human organs affected and the view of physiology rather than the disease itself. Along with precious medicine, it also introduces numerous food ingredients and medicinal herbs that are easily available. The medicinal herbs are written in Chinese characters and also in widely-used *Hangul* (Korean writing system) names so commoners could easily recognize the different herbs. The book emphasized the prevention of illness by controlling one's diet and eating well to protect the body rather than trying to heal an already developed illness.

Donguibogam was published and used in many countries, including China and Japan, in that era. The book contains numerous methods for using food ingredients and medicinal herbs based on the philosophy of the *Yin-Yang* Five Elements, and it is still studied and used by doctors of Korean medicine, chefs, and Korean people who are interested in it.

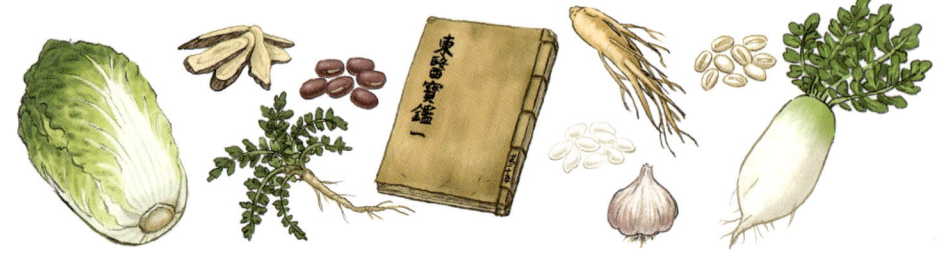

Ingredients for Korean Cuisine

Korea has four distinct seasons and a variety of ingredients.

Grains

Rice, barley, wheat, millet, sorghum, red beans, soybeans, and mung beans are used to cook white rice or multi-grain rice as the main dish.

Fruits

Aside from the popular apples and Asian pears, there are many other fruits enjoyed in each season—strawberries and cherries in the spring; Korean melons, watermelons, and peaches in the summer; grapes, jujubes, and yuzu in the fall; and dried persimmon in the winter. There are also berries, such as Schisandra, used mostly for making drinks, and various nuts, including chestnuts, ginkgo nuts, pine nuts, and walnuts.

Vegetables

Napa cabbage and daikon radishes are the most widely used vegetables. Other seasonal vegetables include lettuce, summer radishes, water parsley, crown daisies, perilla leaves, chilis, carrots, onions, pumpkins, cucumbers, eggplants, bellflower roots, bean sprouts, and mushrooms.

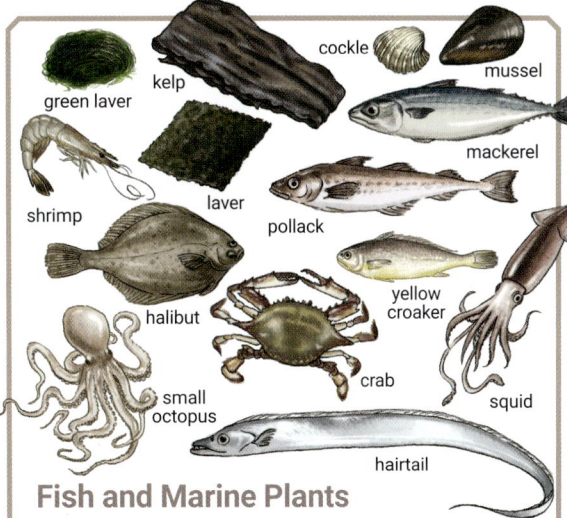

Fish and Marine Plants

A diverse range of seafood is used in Korean cooking, including seaweed, laver, kelp, green laver, pollack, yellow croaker, mackerel, hairtail, cod, Spanish mackerel, halibut, anchovies, squid, octopus, small octopus, shrimp, crabs, and clams.

Meat

 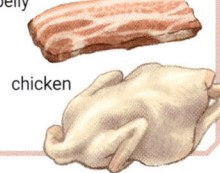

The most beloved meat is beef, but Koreans also enjoy pork and chicken.

Condiments for Korean Cuisine

What is a condiment?
Condiments are the seasoning and spices used in cooking to bring out the natural flavor of the ingredient and remove any unpleasant smell or taste. The Korean word for condiment is *"yangnyeum,"* which means "to keep in mind that it will be beneficial to the body like medicine." The most distinctive and basic condiment for Korean cuisine is *"jang"* of which the most used ones are *ganjang* (soy sauce), *doenjang* (soybean paste), and *gochujang* (red chili paste).

Soy sauce
Soy sauce is the most important and basic condiment for seasoning dishes. Traditionally, *jip-ganjang* (traditional homemade soy sauce) was used at every household, but *yangjo-ganjang* (store-bought soy sauce) is also widely used these days.

Jip-ganjang
Fermented soybean bricks called *meju*, which are made with boiled and ground soybeans, are dried and then aged in brine to make *jip-ganjang*. Also called by many other names, such as *guk-ganjang* (soup soy sauce), *jeontong-ganjang* (traditional soy sauce), *hansik-ganjang*, and Joseon *ganjang*, *jip-ganjang* was traditionally made at home. Nowadays, you can easily find different brands of store-bought soy sauce. *Jip-ganjang* is mostly used for seasoning soups and stews and also added to *namul* (seasoned vegetables) and braised dishes. Some households keep decades old *jip-ganjang* and enjoy it over a long period of time. It is said that the longer it is aged, the darker the color and the healthier it becomes.

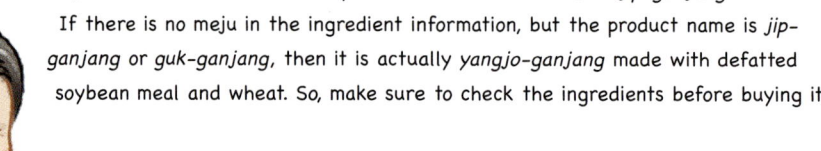

Tips for buying *jip-ganjang*!

Jip-ganjang available in stores have different brand names such as *guk-ganjang* or *jeontong-ganjang*, and they are made with different ingredients, which makes it hard to select the right one. But traditional *jip-ganjang* is made with just three ingredients: *meju* (soybean), water, and salt. If the ingredient list on the product label includes *meju* (soybean), water, salt, and just a few other additives, then the taste will be fairly close to that of traditional *jip-ganjang*.

If there is no meju in the ingredient information, but the product name is *jip-ganjang* or *guk-ganjang*, then it is actually *yangjo-ganjang* made with defatted soybean meal and wheat. So, make sure to check the ingredients before buying it.

Jip-ganjang and *Doenjang* Recipe

18%~20% brine

Soak soybeans and boil them. → Pound in a stone mortar. → Shape into *meju* and dry. → Ferment the *meju*. → Put *meju* inside a clay pot (*hangari*) and pour in salt water.

Ferment for 40 days. → Separate *doenjang* (hard ingredients) from *ganjang* (liquid).

→ Filter *ganjang* to leave only clear liquid. → Store in a clay pot (*hangari*). — *Jip-ganjang*

→ Scoop out the *meju* and pound it. → Put inside a clay pot (*hangari*) and ferment. — *Doenjang*

Yangjo-ganjang

Used for seasoning meat and fish dishes, *yangjo-ganjang* is made by adding *koji* (Aspergillus) to soybean or defatted soybean meals mixed with starch products (rice, barley, wheat) and fermenting it. *Yangjo-ganjang* is mass produced in factories, and along with other factory-made condiments like *doenjang* and *gochujang*, it is inexpensive and easily available. Some products have "*jin-ganjang*" written on the label, but whichever product you select, make sure it is 100% *yangjo-ganjang*.

Doenjang

Doenjang (soybean paste) is the byproduct of *ganjang*, and it is made by fermenting the soy ingredients separated from the *ganjang* liquid. It is used for making *doenjang-guk* (soybean paste soup), *doenjang-jjigae* (soybean paste stew), and *namul*.

It can be homemade or bought from the store or market. Products that are high in soybean and low in additives other than water and salt are recommended.

Gochujang

A mixture of malt water and glutinous rice powder is added to *gochutgaru* (red chili powder), *meju* powder and salt and fermented to make this spicy traditional *jang*. Homemade or store-bought *gochujang* is used to season spicy dishes. Store-bought products made with *meju* powder and malt will taste similar to traditional *gochujang*. Just make sure to check the level of spiciness before buying it.

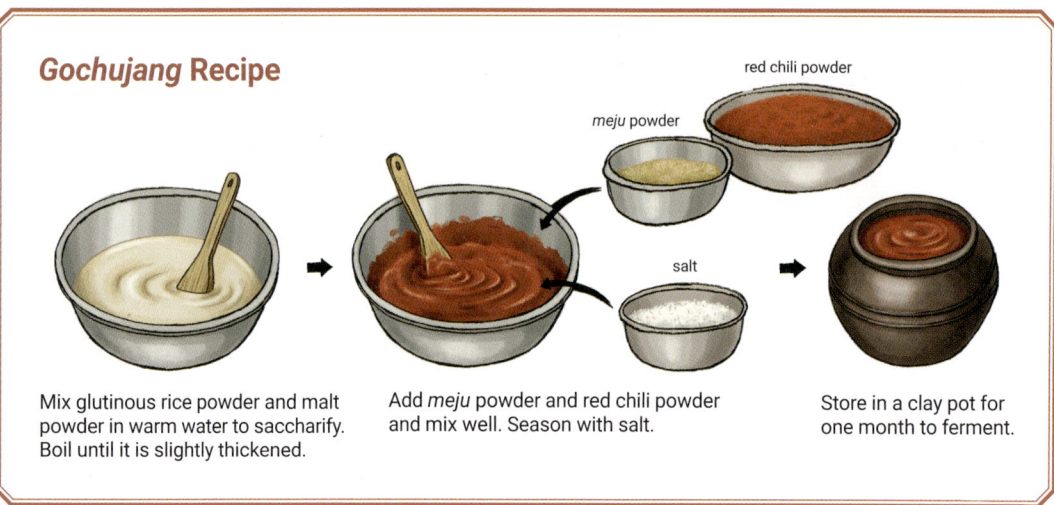

Gochujang Recipe

Mix glutinous rice powder and malt powder in warm water to saccharify. Boil until it is slightly thickened.

Add *meju* powder and red chili powder and mix well. Season with salt.

Store in a clay pot for one month to ferment.

Ssamjang

This *jang* is added to lettuce or napa cabbage wraps or used as a dipping sauce for grilled meat dishes.

Doenjang and *gochujang* are mixed together, and then minced garlic, green onions, sesame oil, sesame seeds, and honey or sugar are added to make this condiment. You can also use store-bought *ssamjang*.

Salt
Koreans use *cheonilyeom* for cooking, which is a natural sea salt made by evaporating moisture from sea water with wind and the sun. Large and flaky *cheonilyeom* is used for brining the cabbage and radish in making kimchi, and refined *cheonilyeom (kkotsogeum)* that is grainier is used for regular cooking.

Gochutgaru
Dried red chilis are ground into coarse or fine powder and used in various recipes.

Cooking Oil
A wide range of cooking oil is used depending on the recipe. Some of these oils are sesame oil, perilla oil, canola oil, corn oil, soybean oil, and cottonseed oil. Sesame oil is made by pressing after toasting sesame seeds, and it has a unique nutty aroma which goes well with Korean cuisine.

Sugar, Honey, Corn Syrup
Corn syrup and *jochung* (traditional grain syrup) are used to sweeten and add shine to dishes.

Vinegar
Apple vinegar, green plum vinegar, and vinegars made from various grain are used.

Black Pepper
Black pepper is used for removing unpleasant smell from meat and fish and help bring out the natural flavor of ingredients.

Fish Sauce
Saeujeot, made by salting and fermenting small shrimp, is used for kimchi and soup dishes. *Myeolchiaekjeot* is fermented anchovy sauce which is used to season kimchi, stew, and soup dishes. Fish sauce made from sand eel can also be used.

Cinnamon
It is usually used for making rice cakes, confections, and beverages.

Sesame Seeds
Toasted sesame seeds are used as a sauce ingredient or garnish.

Ginger
This root vegetable is minced or sliced and added to kimchi, fish, meat dishes, and also traditional confections.

Mustard
Fermented spicy mustard is used as a sauce ingredient. You can also use Korean mustards sold in tubes.

Garlic, Green Onions
A popular Korean ingredient, garlic is minced or used whole. Green onions are cut into various shapes and sizes according to the recipe.

Garnishes for Korean Cuisine

Garnish is the decoration placed on top of dishes to make them more appealing. The garnishes for Korean cuisine adopt their colors from the *Yin-Yang* Five Elements philosophy: white, yellow, blue (green), red, and black.

Basic Cooking Techniques for Korean Cuisine

Mincing

Minced garlic
Peel the garlic and remove the brown top end. Rinse and mince. (You can use a blender, but mincing by hand makes the seasoning more flavorful.)

10 g garlic = 1 Tbsp minced garlic = 3 tsp minced garlic

Minced ginger
Wash and peel the ginger and mince.

7 g ginger = 1 Tbsp minced ginger = 3 tsp minced ginger

Minced green onion
Remove the dirt covered end and mince only the white section.

10 g green onion = 1 Tbsp minced green onion = 3 tsp minced green onion

Making Juice

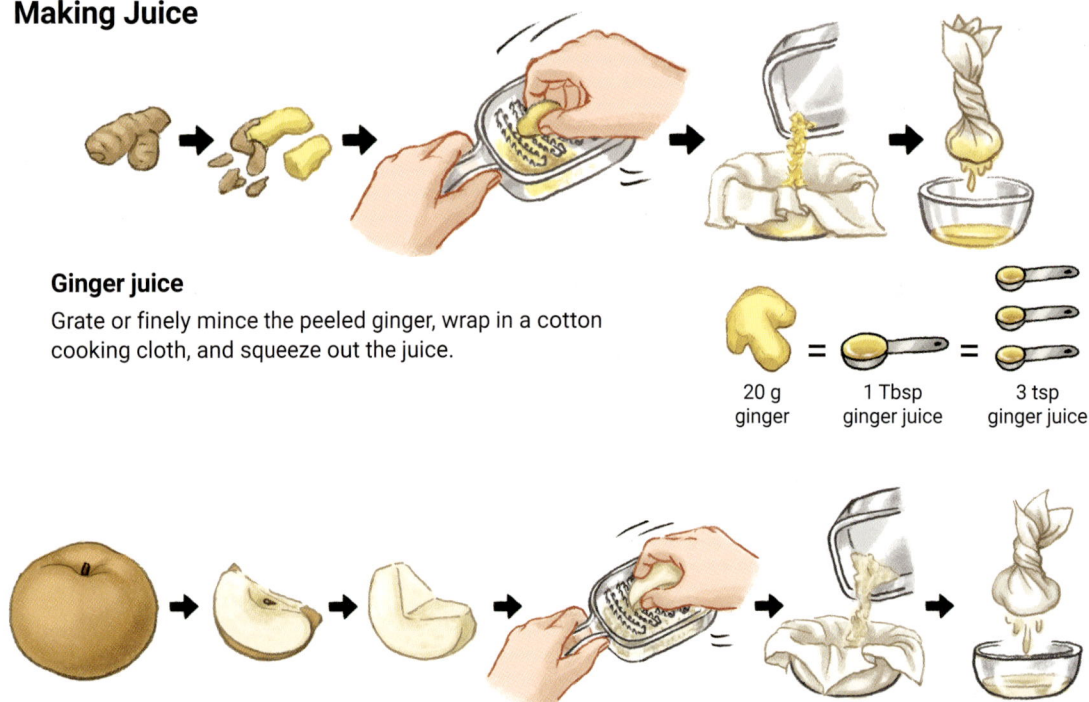

Ginger juice
Grate or finely mince the peeled ginger, wrap in a cotton cooking cloth, and squeeze out the juice.

20 g ginger = 1 Tbsp ginger juice = 3 tsp ginger juice

Asian pear juice
Wash and peel the pear and grate. Wrap in a cotton cooking cloth and squeeze out the juice.

20 g Asian pear = 1 Tbsp pear juice = 3 tsp pear juice

Softening Mung Bean Jelly

Cut the mung bean jelly according to the use.

Blanch the jelly in boiling water for 1 to 2 minutes.

Turn off the heat and leave the jelly in water, which will become soft and translucent.

Cutting

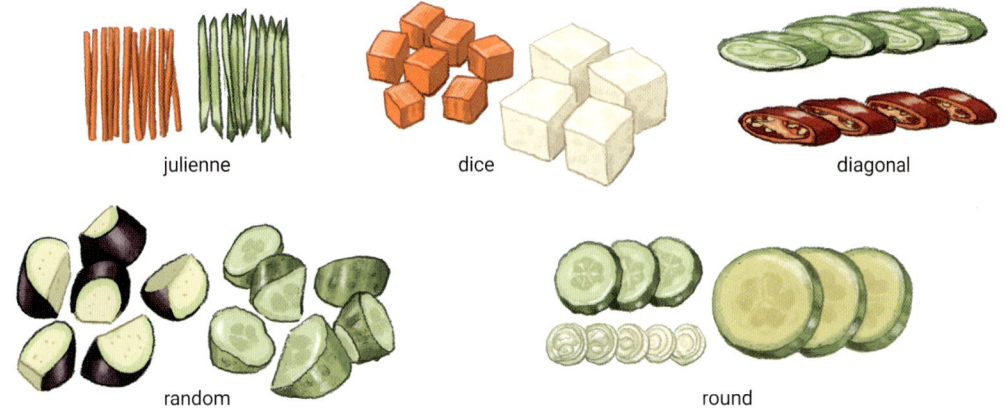

Making *Jidan*

Separate egg white and yolk. Pour egg white over a sieve to loosen it. Stir egg yolk well to loosen as well.

Preheat a frying pan and turn off the heat when the pan is hot. Drizzle some cooking oil and pour out excess oil when it's heated.

When the pan is cooled slightly, pan-fry the egg white and yolk mixtures separately over low heat. Turn over and cook on the other side.

Adjust the thickness of the *jidan* according to the dish. Use thin *jidan* for *gujeolpan*, *guksu-jangguk* and bibimbap, and use thick *jidan* for *sinseollo* and *jeongol*.

Making Toasted Sesame Seeds

Wash uncooked sesame seeds and drain. Slowly toast over medium heat in a relatively deep pot. Grind the toasted sesame seeds using a sesame seed blender or a small mortar and pestle. If using store-bought toasted sesame seeds, make sure it's been recently toasted.

Making Pine Nut Powder

Wipe the pine nuts with a cotton cooking cloth, place on top of *hanji* (Korean traditional paper) or blot paper, and mince with a large knife. The paper will absorb the natural oil, leaving a grainy powder.

Rehydrating Dried Fernbrake

Boil water using an amount that's twice that of the fernbrake, and then add the dried fernbrake.

Boil for 2 minutes.

When the fernbrake is completely submerged, close the lid and turn off the heat. Leave for 1 hour to soften the stems.

Wash 3 times and use for cooking.

You can rehydrate dried bellflower roots, taro stems, and eggplants in the same way.

Measurements used for this cookbook

Weight is measured in grams (g).
1 oz = 28.35 g

Volume is measured in milliliters (ml)
or cubic centimeters (cc).
1 L = 1000 ml (cc)
1 cup = 200 ml (cc)

1 tablespoon (Tbsp/T) = 15 ml (cc)

1 teaspoon (tsp/t) = 5 ml (cc)

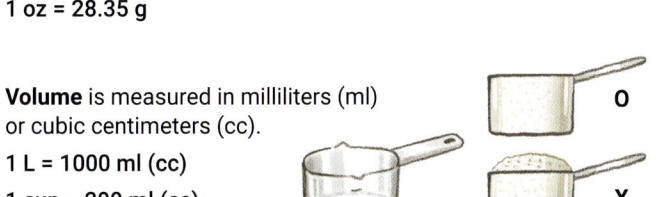
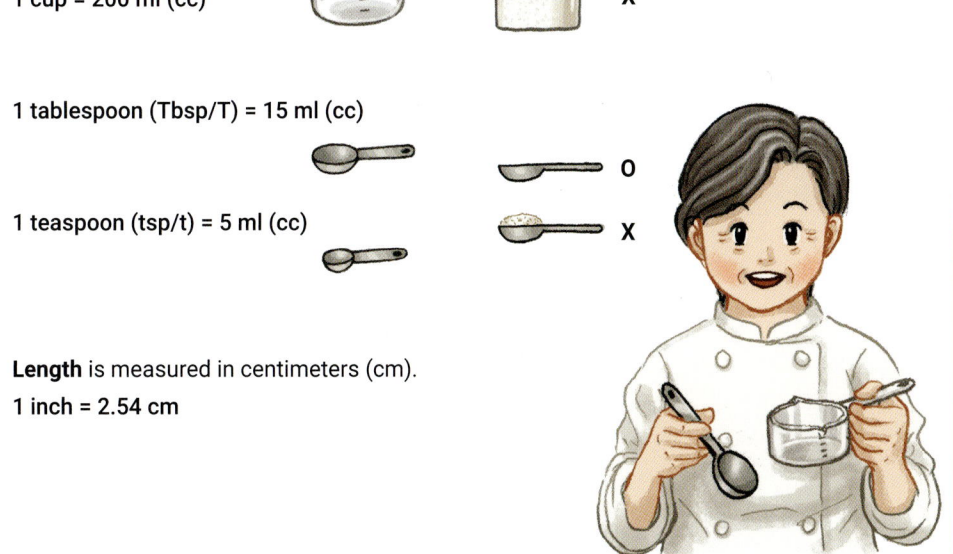

Length is measured in centimeters (cm).
1 inch = 2.54 cm

Main Dish

The main dish for every Korean meal is made with grain, and it is the staple part of Korean cuisine. That is why rice is an important dish in Korean cuisine. Different types of grain are used for cooking, but the most common and popular grain is rice which is cooked as steamed rice or porridge. Wheat flour is also used widely to make noodle and dumpling dishes.

Bap (Rice)

Ogokbap (Steamed Five-grain Rice)

Bibimbap

Gimbap

Hobakjuk (Pumpkin Porridge)

Jatjuk (Pine Nut Porridge)

Guksu-jangguk (Noodles in Hot Beef-based Broth)

Mul-naengmyeon (Cold Buckwheat Noodles)

Mandut-guk (Dumpling Soup)

Chapter 1
Main Dish

Chapter 1
Main Dish

밥
Bap
Rice

White steamed rice, the non-glutinous variety, is a Korean staple food that is central to Korean cuisine. Just like the old saying, "Koreans get their strength from rice," Koreans consider it an important food source. It can be served alongside any kind of side dish known as *banchan*.

Ingredients 4 servings

2 cups of white rice

2 1/2 cups of water

The amount of water that must be added depends on the condition of the rice and the season of the year.

The Japonica variety—with its short, round, hard, and translucent grain—is widely used in Korean cooking. Locally-harvested rice is recommended for its slightly sticky and fluffy texture.

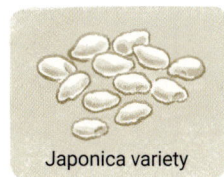 

Japonica variety   Indica variety

Choose rice that has been harvested and milled most recently.

Rice is categorized according to different stages of milling.

 →  →  →  → →

Grain | Brown rice (grain without skins) | *Obundomi* (50% of bran removed) | *Chilbundomi* (70% of bran removed) | White rice (bran completely removed)

Hyeonmi-bap (Brown Rice)

Brown rice is more difficult to digest compared to white rice, but it contains more fiber and vitamin B. Brown rice absorbs less water, so add more water and let it soak for a longer duration than white rice. Chew longer to help with digestion.

Bap (White Rice)

White rice is made with non-glutinous rice without adding any other grain. The texture is soft and it is easy to digest.

Sometimes after scooping out all the rice from the pot, there is a layer of scorched rice stuck to the bottom. This is called *nooroongji*.

Nooroongji can be eaten as it is or deep fried in oil and sprinkled with sugar to make a sweet and crunchy cracker. It's hard to make *nooroongji* with a standard household electric rice cooker, but you can buy packaged *nooroongji* from stores or at the market.

Add water to *nooroongji* and boil to make *soongnyung*.

Soongnyung has a warm nutty flavor that is enjoyed like tea after a meal.

Oh, Mom! Isn't that too much rice?

Didn't you know I get my strength from rice? Chew your rice slowly to taste the sweet flavor.

Chapter 1

Main Dish

오곡밥
Ogokbap

Steamed Five-grain Rice

Ogokbap is made with rice and four other types of grain. It is a seasonal food eaten on Jeongwol Daeboreum, or the first full moon of the Lunar New Year, to ward off bad luck and pray for a good harvest in the coming year. These days, multigrain rice is recommended for its high amounts of nutrients.

Ingredients 4 servings

2 cups of
glutinous rice

1/2 cup of
glutinous millet

1/2 cup of
glutinous sorghum

1/2 cup of
red beans

1/2 cup of
black beans

1 tsp
salt

4 cups of water
(red bean water + water)

White rice, barley, glutinous millet, white soybean, and kidney beans can be used to make *ogokbap*, and the ratio of the grains can be changed according to preference. In Korea, mothers celebrate their children's birthdays with a meal of *miyeok-guk* (seaweed soup) and *chalbap* (rice made with glutinous rice and red bean) in the morning.

white rice

soybeans

kidney beans

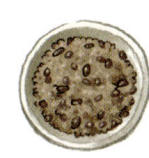
Chalbap
(rice made with
glutinous rice and
red beans)

Miyeok-guk
(seaweed soup)

barley

glutinous millet

1 Wash all the ingredients three times individually.

Soak the glutinous rice for 30 minutes and drain.

2 Soak the black beans for more than 1 hour and drain.

3 Soak the glutinous sorghum for more than 1 hour.

Wash glutinous sorghum by rubbing it between both hands and discard the water. Repeat this 3 to 4 times to remove the red color and drain.

4 Soak the glutinous millet for 30 minutes and drain.

3 cups of water

5 Put the red beans in a large pot and add water to completely cover the beans. When the water boils, discard the water. (Bitterness from the beans seeps out the first time it boils.)

Pour fresh water into the pot and cook the beans until soft while still retaining their shape. Drain and set aside the water for later use.

6 Add all ingredients to a pot except for the glutinous millet. (Glutinous millet is very small and can stick to the bottom of the pot.) Add water, red bean water, and salt into the pot. Close the pot with a lid and cook under high heat.

When the water boils, add the glutinous millet to the top. Lower heat to medium, close the lid, and cook for 5 minutes.

Reduce to low heat and cook for 10 minutes.

Turn off the heat and let it sit for 2 minutes.

Remove the lid and mix the rice several times with a rice paddle.

Scoop it into a bowl to serve.

Jeongwol Daeboreum meal

Jeongwol Daeboreum
(15th of the first lunar month)

Jeongwol Daeboreum is a traditional Korean holiday celebrated on the first full moon on the lunar calendar. People looked up to the full moon and wished for a year of good harvest and well-being. This day was celebrated by having *bokssam* (rice wrapped in toasted laver), *bureom* (various nuts), *namul* (seasoned dried roots and vegetables), *ogokbap* (five-grain rice), and traditional rice wine. This tradition is still practiced today.

Chapter 1
Main Dish

비빔밥
Bibimbap
Bibimbap

Sautéed beef, vegetables, and eggs are mixed with white rice for this dish. It was called *goldongban* in the Joseon court and it was said to be made on the last day of the year. Traditional bibimbap was made with sautéed or blanched vegetables, but various seasonal fresh vegetables can also be added. Meat, fried eggs, and various vegetables, each representing the five symbolic colors, are arranged on top of the rice.

Ingredients 4 servings

2 cups of
white rice

100 g
bellflower root

150 g
Korean zucchini

100 g
mung bean jelly

100 g
rehydrated fernbrake

120 g
beef

1 piece of kelp
(5 cm x 10 cm)

2 eggs

small
pinch of salt

marinade (beef and fernbrake)

1 Tbsp soy sauce
(*yangjo-ganjang*)

1 tsp
sugar

1/2 tsp sesame
seeds

1 tsp minced
green onion

1/2 tsp minced
garlic

1/3 tsp
sesame oil

a small pinch of
black pepper

2 Tbsp
gochujang

1 Tbsp
sesame oil

a drizzle of
cooking oil

a drizzle of
sesame oil

a pinch of
salt

For the green vegetable, *aehobak* (Korean zucchini) can be substituted with zucchini, cucumber, spinach, or water parsley. Instead of the bellflower root, you can use daikon radish, mung bean sprouts, or bean sprouts for the white. Shiitake mushrooms can be used for the brown. There are many different varieties of bibimbap using different ingredients.

yuk-hoe bibimbap
(raw beef bibimbap)

hoe-bibimbap
(raw fish bibimbap)

dolsot-bibimbap
(hot stone pot bibimbap)

saeng-chaeso bibimbap
(fresh vegetable bibimbap)

Beef brisket broth can be used to cook the rice for bibimbap. The rice soaks up the savory flavor, enhancing the overall taste.

1 Soak the rice for 30 minutes and cook. (See p. 28.)

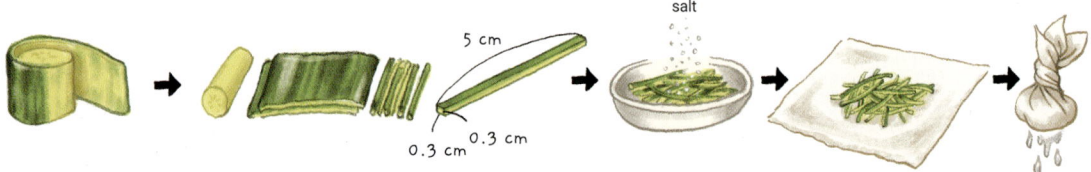

2 Julienne zucchini.
(Don't use the seed-filled part in the middle.)

Add a pinch of salt and brine for 10 minutes. Wrap it in a cotton cooking cloth and squeeze out the water.

3 Peel the bellflower root and julienne. Sprinkle salt and rub lightly with a hand under water to remove the bitter taste. (You can use dried store-bought bellflower root. See p. 22.)

4 Julienne the beef and marinate it.

5 Cut off the hard part of the rehydrated fernbrake and divide into 5 cm pieces and marinate it. (You can use dried store-bought fernbrake after rehydrating. See p. 22 for rehydrating dried fernbrake.)

Make condiments.

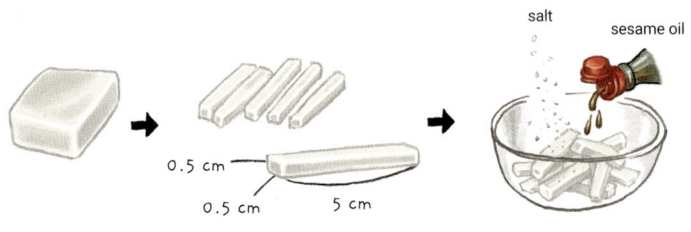

6 Julienne mung bean jelly and season with salt and sesame oil. (If the jelly is too hard, blanch in boiling water to soften it. See p. 20.)

7 Separate egg white and yolk and pan-fry to make *jidan* and julienne into thin strips. (See p. 21 for making *jidan*.)

8 On an oiled pan, sauté the ingredients separately in the following order: bellflower root, zucchini, beef.

Gently sauté the fernbrake by adding a little bit of water as it cooks.

9 Fry dried kelp in oil and crush into small pieces.

10 Arrange the cooked ingredients on top of the rice and add the fried kelp and eggs. Serve with *gochujang* and sesame oil.

Add *gochujang* and sesame oil according to taste. For those who don't prefer spicy food, add soy sauce instead of *gochujang*. Traditionally, *jip-ganjang* was used to season bibimbap.

Chapter 1
Main Dish

김밥
Gimbap
Gimbap

Roll the rice with beef and assorted vegetables and cut it into bite-size pieces for this simple dish. Change the ingredients to make your own favorite gimbap. This easy-to-eat finger food is the perfect meal you can have on-the-go. It is a popular picnic food for everyone.

Ingredients 4 rolls of gimbap

2 cups of white rice	1 Tbsp sesame oil	1/2 tsp salt	2 eggs	1/2 cucumber	60 g burdock
60 g carrot	60 g sweet pickled radish	50 g Korean style ham	40 g fish cake	4 sheets of laver	

jorim-ganjang (flavored soy sauce)

2 Tbsp soy sauce (*yangjo-ganjang*) | 1 1/2 Tbsp sugar | 2 Tbsp water | small pinch of salt | a drizzle of cooking oil

Make sure the gimbap rice isn't cooked to a sticky texture. Add a mixture made with vinegar, sugar, and salt to add flavor and prevent it from going bad.
Avoid ingredients that contains too much moisture.
Cheese and ham, as well as tuna, beef, and kimchi, are used as popular fillings. Ingredients hard to find can be left out.

I like *ggoma* (mini) gimbap with carrots, sweet pickled radish, and spinach. *Chungmu*-gimbap made with spicy squid and radish is also delicious!

Beef or tuna? I can't decide.

My favorite is cheese gimbap!

chamchi (tuna) gimbap   *sogogi* (beef) gimbap   cheese gimbap

ggoma (mini) gimbap

chungmu-gimbap

rice: water = 1 : 1.2 (volume)

1 Wash rice and let it soak for 30 minutes.

Cook rice. (See p. 28.)

Season cooked rice.

2 Add salt to the egg and beat well. Pan fry it into a long thick omelet and cut into long strips.

3 Julienne burdock into long strips. Wash and drain.

4 Thinly slice the fish cake in the same length as the laver.

5 Simmer the *yangjo-ganjang* mixture in a pot. Add the burdock and boil down until a teaspoon of sauce is left in the pot.

Put the burdock to the side and lightly sauté fish cake in the remaining sauce.

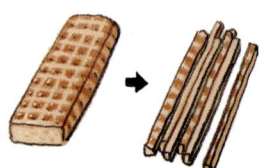

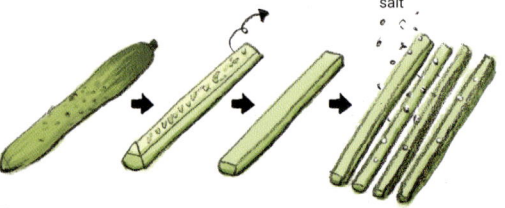

6 Thinly slice the ham in the same length as the laver.

7 Thinly slice the cucumber in the same length and remove the seeds. Lightly salt the cucumber to bring out the water and squeeze out water.

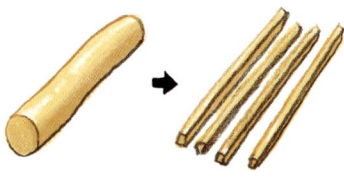

8 Thinly slice the sweet pickled radish lengthwise. (You can use store-bought pickled radish that is already cut into strips for gimbap.)

9 Julienne the carrot into long strips.

Sauté the carrot strips in an oiled pan with salt.

10 Lightly toast the laver without oil. (You can use store-bought toasted laver for gimbap making.)

11 Place the laver, rough side facing up and spread the rice evenly covering 3/4 of the surface.

Lay the prepared ingredients on top of the rice and roll from the bottom, putting firm pressure over the roll with the help of a mat, if using one.

12 To prevent the rice from sticking to the knife, evenly coat both sides of the blade with a few drops of sesame oil and cut the roll into 1 cm thick pieces. Serve on a plate with the fillings facing up.

Chapter 1
Main Dish

호박죽·잣죽

Hobakjuk·Jatjuk

Pumpkin Porridge·Pine Nut Porridge

Pumpkin porridge is made with sweet pumpkin and glutinous rice. The sweet, velvety porridge is recommended for the elderly and recovering patients or it can be served as an appetizer before the main dish. It is a popular porridge in Korea.

Pine nuts and white rice is cooked to make this easy-to-digest, aromatic porridge. It was served before breakfast in the Joseon court.

Ingredients 2 servings

Hobakjuk

 1/2 sweet pumpkin (500 g)
 1/2 cup of glutinous rice powder
 1/2 tsp salt
 1–2 Tbsp sugar
 4 cups of water

Jatjuk

 1 cup of pine nuts
 1/2 cup of white rice
 5 cups of water
 a drizzle of salt

> It is important to finely grind the rice and pine nuts together and to continuously stir with a wooden spoon while cooking to bring out the nutty flavor. Adding salt during cooking can ruin the porridge, so make sure to season at the very end.

In the old days, large and not-too-sweet mature pumpkins were used for making pumpkin porridge, but small sweet pumpkins are more widely used these days. You can add red beans and other ingredients to make *hobak-beombeok* (dried porridge).

pine nut

It is written in *Donguibogam* that "pine nuts brighten the skin and fatten the five main organs of the body and gives energy to weakened areas." Pine nut porridge was considered a nutritious food from old days.

neulgeun-hobak (mature sweet pumpkin)

dan-hobak (sweet pumpkin)

Pumpkin Porridge

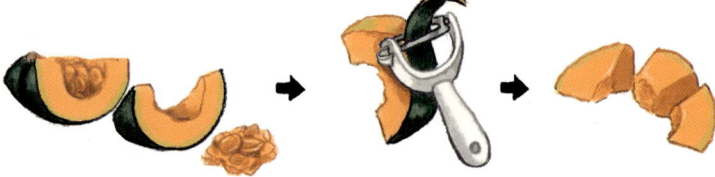

1 Remove seeds, peel skin, and cut into large chunks.

2 Add pumpkin and water to a thick pot and boil.

Reduce to medium heat and cook for 20 minutes.

Mash pumpkin in the pot.

3 Mix glutinous rice powder with water. (You can use starch instead of rice powder.)

Slowly add it to the pot, stirring well as it simmers.

4 When the consistency is right, season with salt and sugar.

Pine Nut Porridge

1 Wash rice and soak for 30 minutes.

Blend it with water and purée into a smooth consistency.

Pour over a sieve.

2 Remove the tops.

Wash and soak for a few minutes.

Blend it with water and purée into a smooth consistency.

Pour over a sieve.

Cook over medium heat, stirring with a wooden spoon. When it simmers, cook for 5 minutes more.

3 Slowly add the rice purée into the pot. Continue to stir.

When it simmers, reduce heat to low and cook for 10 minutes. Season with salt and turn off the heat.

Sugar or honey is optional.

Chapter 1
Main Dish

국수장국
Guksu-jangguk
Noodles in Hot Beef-based Broth

This is a hot noodle dish with soup made with beef broth. The long noodle symbolized longevity in Korean culture, making this noodle soup a popular dish served to guests on special occasions including weddings, birthdays, and 60th birthday celebrations. This is why it is also known as *janchi-guksu* (feast noodles).

Ingredients 2 servings

 200 g thin noodles

 50 g beef

 1 egg

 50 g Korean zucchini

 a pinch of chili thread

 a drizzle of cooking oil

 a pinch of salt

broth

 1 piece of kelp (5 cm x 10 cm)

 100 g beef brisket

 5 cm green onion (white part)

 2 cloves garlic

 5 cups of water

 2 tsp soy sauce (*jip-ganjang*)

beef marinade

 1 tsp soy sauce (*yangjo-ganjang*)

 1/3 tsp sugar

 1 tsp minced green onion

 1 tsp minced garlic

 a pinch of sesame seeds

 a pinch of black pepper

 a drizzle of sesame oil

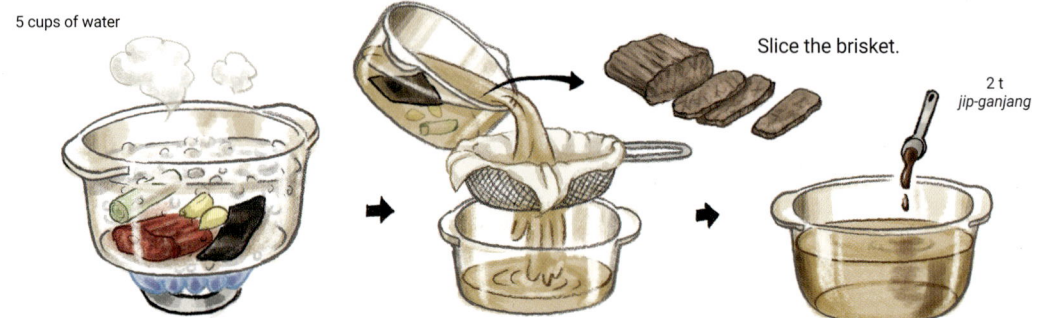

1 Add brisket, kelp, green onion and garlic to a large pot and boil in high heat. When it boils reduce to low heat and cook for 20 minutes.

Remove the brisket and pour the broth through a colander into another pot.

Season broth with *jip-ganjang*.

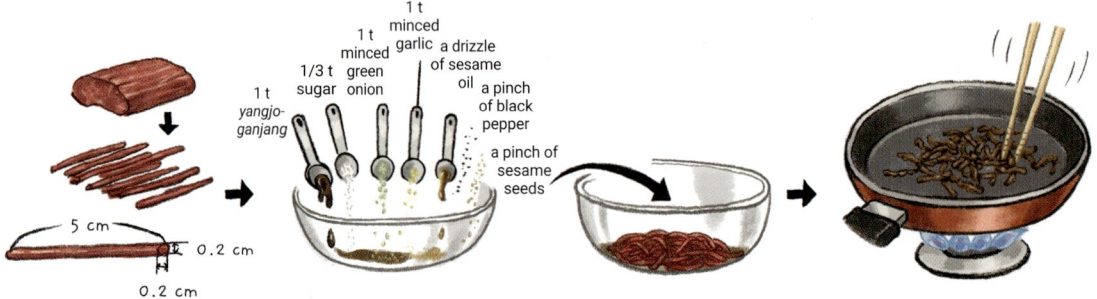

2 Julienne the beef and add marinade sauce. Sauté over medium heat.

3 Julienne the zucchini leaving out the middle seed part and lightly salt them to draw out the water.

Squeeze out the water from the zucchini using a cotton cooking cloth and lightly stir-fry on an oiled pan.

4 Separate egg white and yolk and make *jidan*. Julienne into 5 cm strips. (See p. 21.)

5 Boil enough water in a pot and add noodles. When the water boils again, add 1 cup of cold water and stir noodles to separate them.

When the noodles are cooked, drain quickly and wash them under cold water several times.

Place the noodles in a colander to drain. Twist the noodles into small mounds and place them in a serving bowl. (See p. 53 for noodle mound.)

Pour hot broth over the noodles.

chili thread
white egg *jidan*
yellow egg *jidan*
stir-fried beef
zucchini
sliced brisket

Arrange a small amount of each topping on top of the noodles.

Let's make *bibim-guksu!*

sauce 2 servings

1 1/2 Tbsp *yangjo-ganjang*, 1 tsp sugar,
1 Tbsp sesame oil, 1 tsp sesame seeds

Mix this sauce to the cooked noodles. For a spicier taste, reduce *yangjo-ganjang* and add that much *gochujang*.

Chapter 1
Main Dish

물냉면
Mul-naengmyeon
Cold Buckwheat Noodles

For this cold noodle dish, buckwheat noodles are garnished with pickled cucumbers, radish, hard-boiled eggs, and *pyeonyuk* (boiled and pressed beef), and it is served in a clear, cold beef broth. Beef broth and *dongchimi* (radish water kimchi) liquid can be mixed for added flavor. *Naengmyeon* is originally from the northern part of Korea, but it is now enjoyed throughout the country. *Mul-naengmyeon* refers to *Pyeongyang-naengmyeon*, which is from a city called Pyeongyang in North Korea.

Ingredients 2 servings

| 300 g naengmyeon buckwheat noodles | 1/3 cucumber (50 g) | 100 g daikon radish | 50 g Asian pear | 1 egg |

vinegar mixture

| 2 Tbsp vinegar | 2 Tbsp sugar | 1 tsp salt | 2 Tbsp water |

beef broth

| 100 g beef brisket | 10 cm green onion | 2 cloves garlic | 5 cups of water |

| 2 tsp salt | 1 Tbsp sugar | 2 tsp vinegar | a drizzle of soy sauce (*jip-ganjang*) |

mustard sauce

| 2 Tbsp mustard seed powder | 1 Tbsp warm water | 1 Tbsp vinegar | 1 Tbsp sugar | 1/4 tsp salt |

Hamheung-naengmyeon

This is another popular *naengmyeon* in Korea that is originally from Hamheung, North Korea. Commonly known as *bibim-naengmyeon*, it is mixed in a red, spicy sauce. It is also called *hoe-naengmyeon* as small pieces of raw fish are added.

Here's the recipe for *bibim-naengmyeon*.

Pour sauce over cooked noodles. → Top with the garnish and mix.

sauce 2 servings

50 g onion, 30 g apple, 2 cloves garlic, 5 cm green onion, 1 Tbsp *gochujang*, 3 Tbsp *gochutgaru*, 2 Tbsp honey, 1 Tbsp sugar, 3 Tbsp vinegar, 1/2 Tbsp salt
Mix all ingredients in a blender.

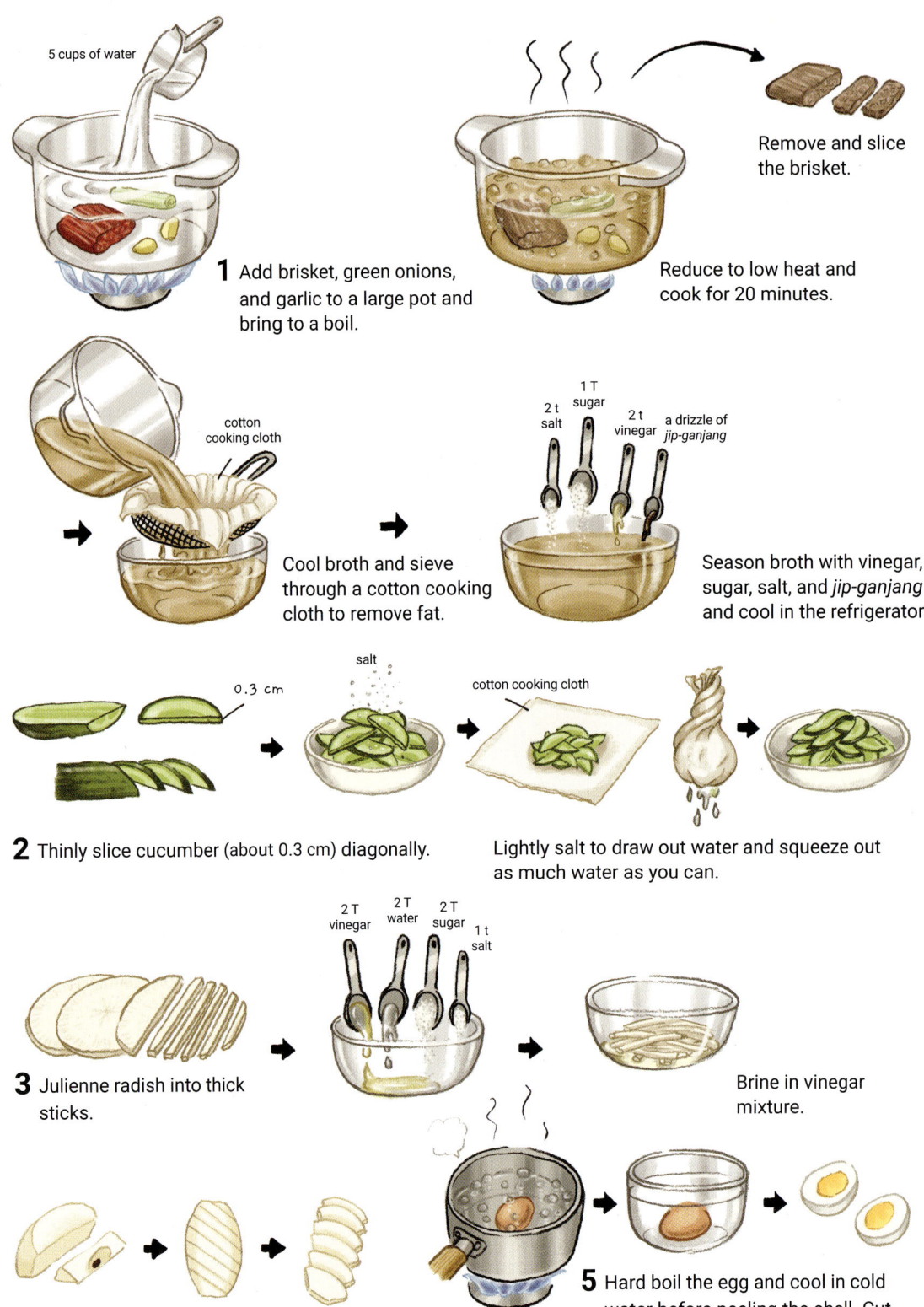

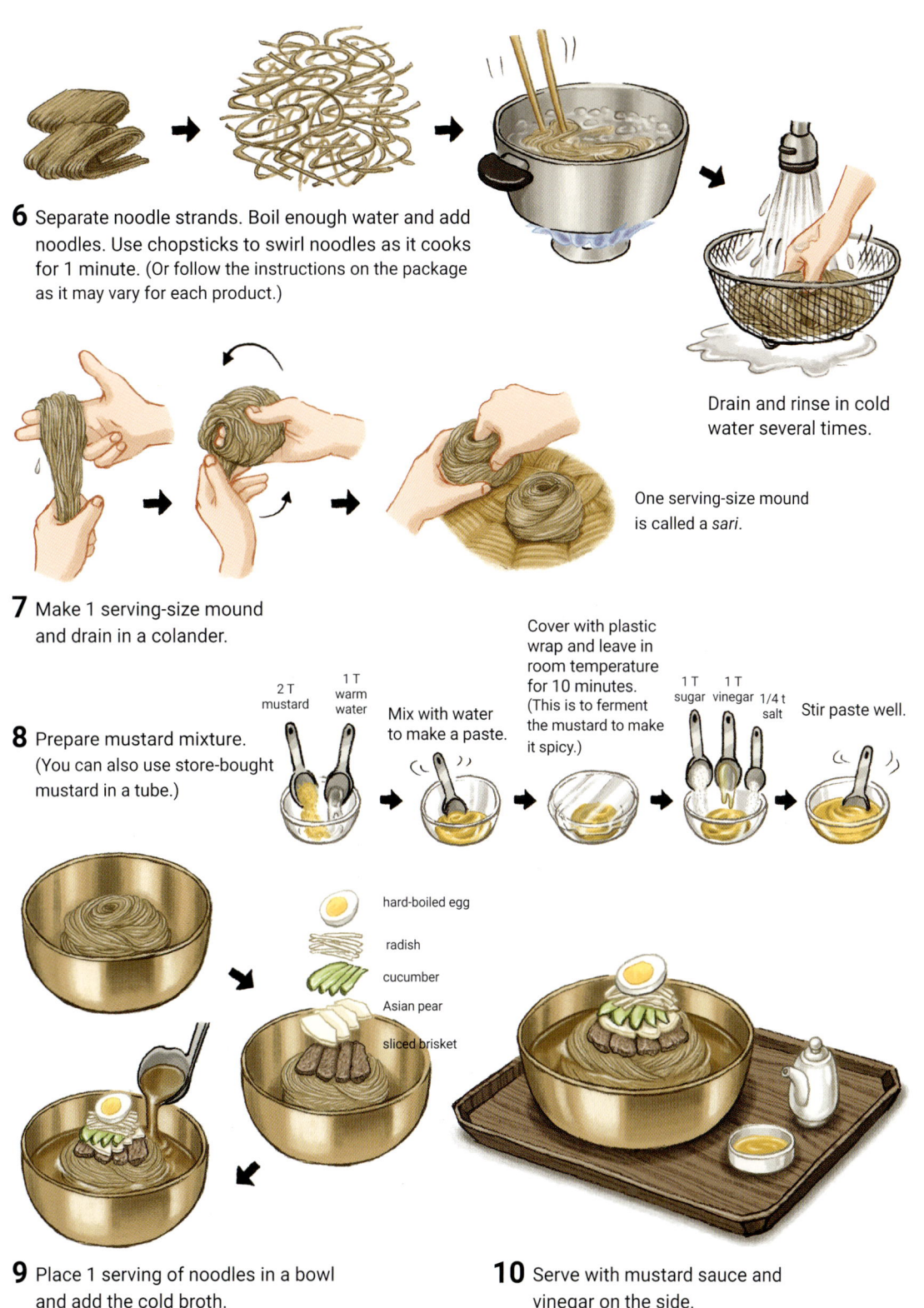

6 Separate noodle strands. Boil enough water and add noodles. Use chopsticks to swirl noodles as it cooks for 1 minute. (Or follow the instructions on the package as it may vary for each product.)

Drain and rinse in cold water several times.

One serving-size mound is called a *sari*.

7 Make 1 serving-size mound and drain in a colander.

8 Prepare mustard mixture. (You can also use store-bought mustard in a tube.)

2 T mustard · 1 T warm water · Mix with water to make a paste. · Cover with plastic wrap and leave in room temperature for 10 minutes. (This is to ferment the mustard to make it spicy.) · 1 T sugar · 1 T vinegar · 1/4 t salt · Stir paste well.

hard-boiled egg
radish
cucumber
Asian pear
sliced brisket

9 Place 1 serving of noodles in a bowl and add the cold broth.

10 Serve with mustard sauce and vinegar on the side.

Chapter 1
Main Dish

만둣국
Mandut-guk

Dumpling Soup

Dumplings filled with beef, pork, and vegetables are cooked in a beef broth to make this warm dumpling soup. It was a traditional Lunar New Year's Day dish in the northern region, but now it is enjoyed throughout the country all year round. Add sliced rice cakes to make *tteokmandut-guk* (rice cake dumpling soup).

Ingredients 2 servings

| 1 1/2 cups of flour | 1/3 tsp salt | 1/2 cup of water | 150 g minced beef | 10 g dried shiitake mushroom | 100 g napa cabbage |

| 100 g mung bean sprouts | 40 g onion | 50 g tofu | 2 eggs | 1/2 Tbsp pine nuts | 1 Tbsp sesame oil |

broth

| 200 g beef brisket | 10 cm green onion (white part) | 3 cloves garlic | 6 cups of water | 1 Tbsp soy sauce (*jip-ganjang*) |

marinade (beef & mushroom)

| 1 Tbsp soy sauce (*yangjo-ganjang*) | 1/2 tsp salt | 1 Tbsp minced green onion | 1 tsp minced garlic | 1/2 tsp sugar | 1 tsp sesame oil | a pinch of black pepper |

dipping sauce (soy-vinegar)

| 2 Tbsp soy sauce (*yangjo-ganjang*) | 1 Tbsp vinegar | 1/2 tsp sugar | a small pinch of *gochutgaru* |

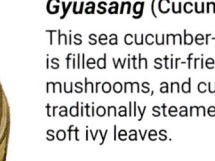

Jjin-mandu (Steamed Dumplings)
Cook the dumplings in a steamer.

Gyuasang (Cucumber Dumplings)
This sea cucumber-shaped dumpling is filled with stir-fried beef, shiitake mushrooms, and cucumber and traditionally steamed on top of soft ivy leaves.

Pyeonsu (Zucchini Dumplings)
The filling is made with beef, Korean zucchini, and shiitake mushrooms and sealed in a pyramid shape. It can be steamed or boiled in beef broth.

1 Add beef brisket, green onion, and garlic in a pot and boil over high heat.

Reduce to medium heat and cook for 20 minutes.

Remove brisket and julienne into short strips. Cool the broth and pour over a colander to remove the impurities.

2 Add salt and water to the flour and knead to make dough. (You can also use store-bought dumpling wrappers, but wrappers made from scratch are chewier and taste better.)

Wrap the dough in a plastic bag and set aside for 20 minutes to rest.

3 Marinate minced beef.

4 Soak dried shiitake mushrooms in hot water to rehydrate and julienne into thin 1 cm pieces.

Marinate and sauté in a pan.

5 Blanch mung bean sprouts and napa cabbage and rinse in cold water.

Squeeze out the water (but not too much) and julienne.

6 Mince onion and lightly sprinkle with salt. Squeeze out the water.

7 Wrap tofu in a cotton cooking cloth and squeeze out the water.

8 Add all ingredients and half an egg to a bowl and mix well. Season with salt.

9 Separate egg white and yolk and make *jidan*. Cut into diamond shapes. (See p. 21.)

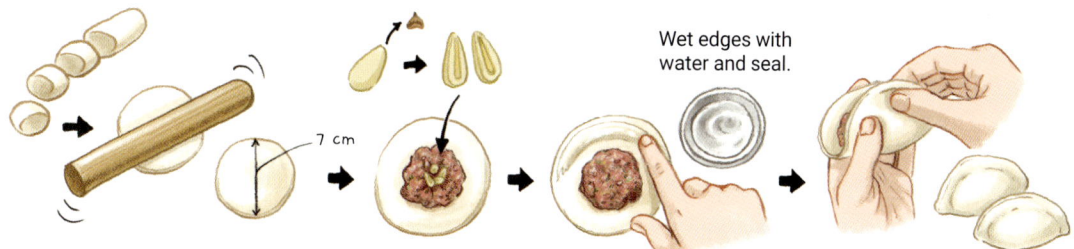

10 Roll dough into small balls and use a rolling pin to flatten into 7 cm circles. Make 20 of them.

Scoop filling onto the wrap and add 3 to 4 pine nut halves. Close and seal wrap into a half-moon shape.

11 Boil beef broth and season with *jip-ganjang*.

Ladle into individual bowls and garnish with the julienned brisket and egg *jidan*. Serve with soy-vinegar dipping sauce.

Side Dish

Guk

Koreans enjoy soup dishes with their meal. A typical Korean table is set with rice, soup, and several side dishes. Soups are made with various vegetables, fish and meat. There are many different kinds of soup dishes using different cooking methods. *Malgeun-jangguk* is a clear soup seasoned with soy sauce, *gom-guk* is made by slow cooking meat or fish in water, *tojang-guk* is seasoned with *doenjang* (soybean paste) or *gochujang* (red chili paste), and *naeng-guk* is a cold soup dish.

Sogogimut-guk (Beef and Radish Soup)

Miyeok-guk (Seaweed Soup)

Sigeumchi Doenjang-guk (Spinach Soybean Paste Soup)

Chapter 2
Side Dish
Guk

Chapter 2
Side Dish
Guk

소고기뭇국
Sogogimut-guk

Beef and Radish Soup

Thinly-sliced radish and seasoned beef are sautéed in a pot and boiled with kelp broth. This easy-to-make recipe is a popular homecooked dish. It has a refreshing and savory flavor that tastes best when it's made with winter radish. The soup is clear when cooked, but add *gochutgaru* when sautéing the radish and beef for a spicy version.

Ingredients 2 servings

| 100 g beef brisket | 150 g daikon radish | 1/2 green onion (white part) | 1 piece of kelp (10 cm x 10 cm) | 5 cups of water | 1 1/2 Tbsp soy sauce (*jip-ganjang*) |

marinade

| 1 Tbsp soy sauce (*jip-ganjang*) | 1 Tbsp minced green onion | 1/2 Tbsp minced garlic | 1 tsp sesame seeds | 2 tsp sesame oil | a small pinch of black pepper |

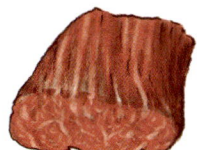

Beef Brisket

Beef brisket is recommended for the broth. Brisket is a cut from the breast section to the underside of the belly. Because it is a tough cut of meat, it's best when boiled rather than grilled. A quick method to use while making broth with brisket is to cut the meat into bite-size pieces, sauté, and boil in water. You can apply this to *miyeok-guk* and *sogogimut-guk*. To get a clear, deep-flavored broth, boil the chunk of meat starting from cold water and pour over a cotton cooking cloth to remove impurities (refer to brisket broth method for *mandut-guk* on p. 56). Kelp can be added to the broth for extra umami flavor. This is suitable for *toran-tang* and *juksun malgeun-tang*.

Toran-tang (Taro Soup)

Peeled taro is boiled in water and cooked in the brisket broth for this soup. Taro comes out in markets around the Korean Thanksgiving season, and it is a traditional Thanksgiving Day dish in the Seoul region.

Juksun Malgeun-tang (Bamboo Shoot Soup)

Tender bamboo shoot harvested in the spring is boiled in brisket broth. There's a first spring vegetable crunchiness in the soup.

Daikon Radish

One of the most widely used vegetables in Korea, it is cooked in various ways including being fermented to make kimchi and *kkakdugi*, seasoned, boiled to make a soup or braised. Radish aids indigestion, and it is a popular hangover food.

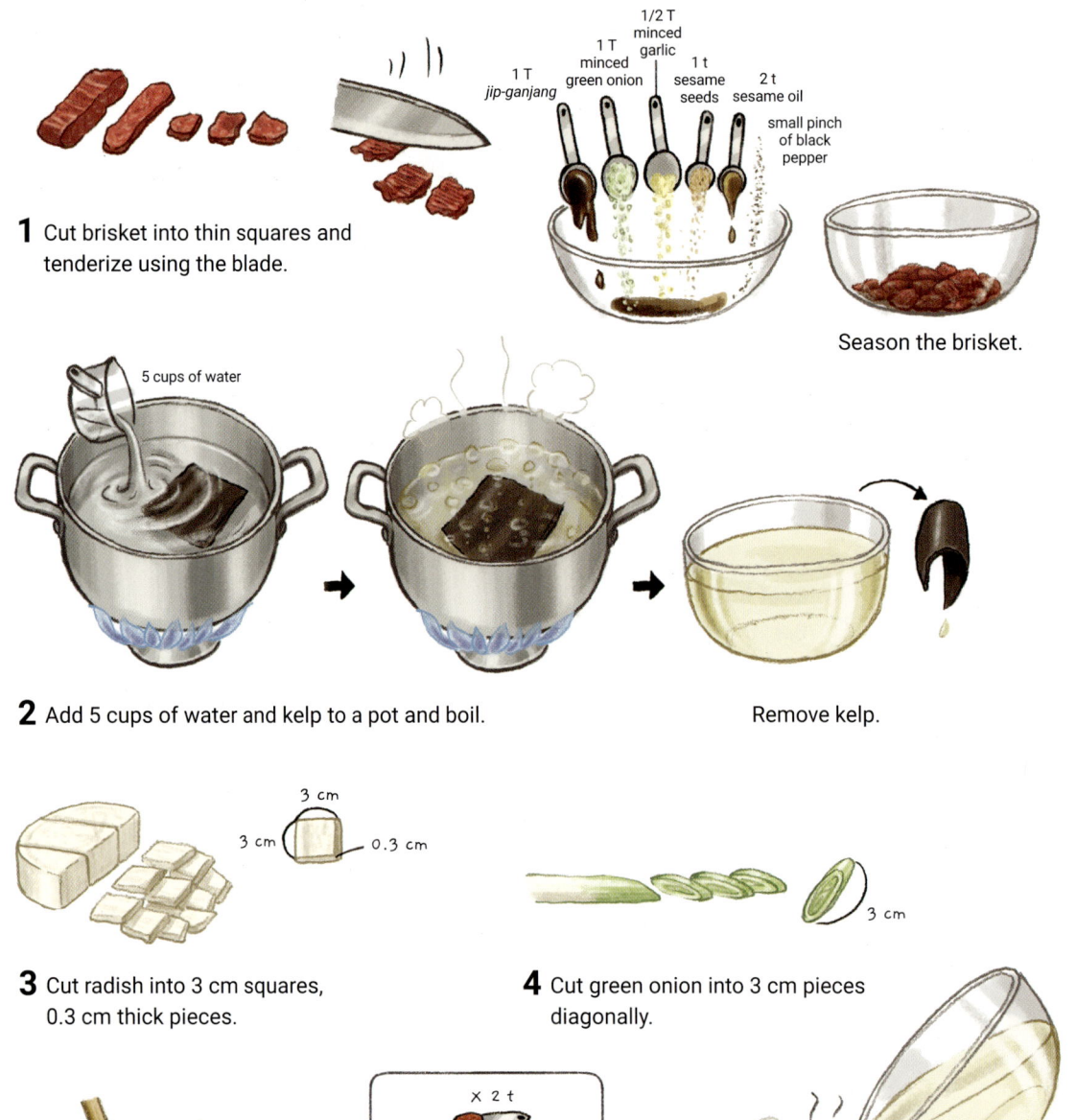

1 Cut brisket into thin squares and tenderize using the blade.

Season the brisket.

2 Add 5 cups of water and kelp to a pot and boil.

Remove kelp.

3 Cut radish into 3 cm squares, 0.3 cm thick pieces.

4 Cut green onion into 3 cm pieces diagonally.

Add 2 tsp *gochutgaru* at this stage to make it spicy.

5 Sauté radish and beef in a pot.

When cooked, add kelp broth and bring to a boil.

6 Reduce to medium heat and cook for 20 minutes. Remove the foam on the top with a ladle.

When the soup becomes clear, add green onions. Season with *jip-ganjang*.

1 1/2 T *jip-ganjang*

Yukgaejang
(Spicy Beef Soup)

Add vegetables to *sogogimut-guk* to make this spicy beef soup.

  Beef, mung bean sprouts, taro stems, fernbrake, green onions, and *gochutgaru* is cooked in the brisket broth.

Mmmm~~ Grandma's *sogogimut-guk* is the best!

Mmmm~~ Mom's *yukgaejang* is the best!

Chapter 2
Side Dish
Guk

미역국
Miyeok-guk
Seaweed Soup

Dried seaweed is rehydrated in water and boiled with beef for this dish. It is a staple soup for new moms after giving birth and is the main dish on the 100th day celebrations of newborns and on birthdays.

Ingredients 2 servings

30 g
dried seaweed

100 g
beef brisket

2 Tbsp soy sauce
(*jip-ganjang*)

2 Tbsp
sesame oil

6 cups of
water

It is a Korean tradition for mothers to eat *miyeok-guk* after giving birth. According to *Donguibogam*, "miyeok (seaweed) eases inner heat, enhances the flow of energy and helps discharge body waste." Therefore, eating seaweed after giving birth helps to ease any swelling. But the health benefits of seaweed make this a recommended food for everyone. It is rich in calcium and iodine, and the natural fiber helps with bowel movement.

Season *miyeok-guk* and other Korean soups with *jip-ganjang* for an authentic Korean flavor.

miyeok
(seaweed)

dried seaweed

65

1 Rehydrate dried seaweed for 20 minutes in water.   Wash well.

Cut into 5 cm lengths and drain.

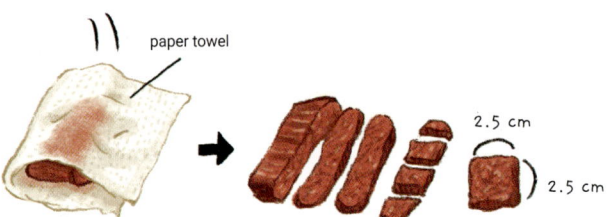

2 Blot the blood from the beef with paper towel and slice thinly.

3 Sauté beef with sesame oil.   When the beef changes in color, add seaweed and sauté until it softens.   Add water and boil.

Reduce to medium heat and cook for 15 minutes. Season with *jip-ganjang*. Reduce to low heat and cook for 5 minutes.

Make **miyeongnaeng-guk (chilled seaweed soup)** in the summer!

ingredients 2 servings

10 g dried seaweed, 1/2 cucumber, 2 tsp soy sauce (*jip-ganjang*), 3 cups of water, 1 Tbsp vinegar

seasoning

1 tsp soy sauce (*jip-ganjang*), 1 tsp minced green onion, 1 tsp minced garlic, 1 tsp sugar, 1 tsp sesame oil, 1/2 tsp sesame seeds

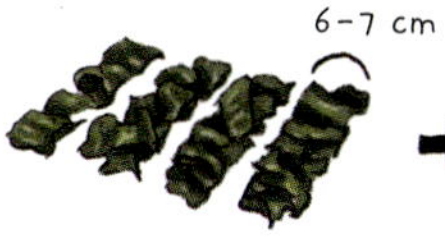

Rehydrate seaweed, wash and cut into 6 cm to 7 cm lengths.

Boil 3 cups of water and cool. Add *jip-ganjang* to the water and transfer to the refrigerator.

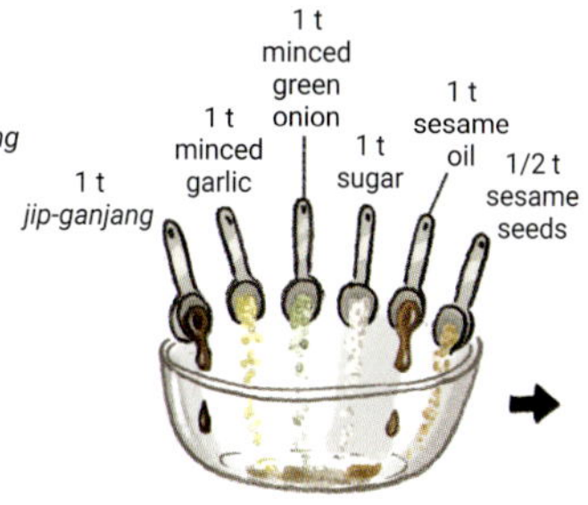

Combine the seasoning.

Julienne cucumber and season.

Mix cucumber and seaweed in a bowl.

Pour the cold liquid in the bowl.

Add vinegar just before serving.

Chapter 2
Side Dish
Guk

시금치된장국
Sigeumchi Doenjang-guk
Spinach Soybean Paste Soup

Anchovy broth is seasoned with *doenjang* (soybean paste) and spinach is added to make this soup. Other ingredients, such as beef and clams, can be used. Season with *doenjang*, *gochujang*, *jip-ganjang*, or salt.

Ingredients 2 servings

150 g
spinach

20 g
dried anchovies for broth

1 piece of kelp
(5 cm x 10 cm)

4 cups of water

5 cm
green onion

1 Tbsp *doenjang*
(soybean paste)

1/2 tsp
minced garlic

a drizzle of soy sauce
(*jip-ganjang*)

Made with vegetables, fish, and beef, *guk* is a thin soup that has more liquid than solid ingredients. Served alongside a bowl of rice, it is an essential part of the Korean meal. You can also use curled mallow, chard or winter cabbage for this soup.

curled mallow

chard

winter cabbage

Myeolchi (Anchovy)

Anchovies are either fermented in salt to make fish sauce or dried for various uses. Dried anchovies are cooked differently depending on the size. Small anchovies are stir-fried and large anchovies are used for making broth. Rich in calcium, dried anchovies can be used as whole.

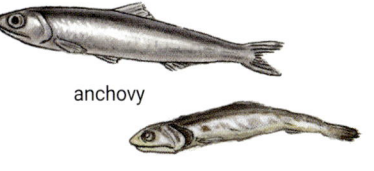

anchovy

dried anchovy

1 Remove wilted leaves and roots, wash, and cut into two or three sections.

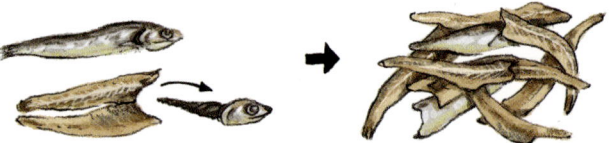

2 Remove anchovy heads and intestines.

3 Add water, anchovies, and kelp in a pot and boil. Turn off the heat after 1 to 2 minutes and use a sieve to remove the solid ingredients, leaving a clear broth.

4 Mix *doenjang* into the broth and boil. Add spinach and cook for 5 minutes.

5 Add sliced green onions and minced garlic and cook for 2 minutes.

Season with *jip-ganjang*.

Make **doenjang-jjigae** with anchovy broth! See p. 15–16 for more information on *doenjang*.

Grandma~ Please put a lot of *chadolbagi* into the *jjigae*~~!

Doenjang-jjigae (Soybean Paste Stew)

Jjigae is a stew dish that has more solid ingredients than liquid. This is an all-time favorite Korean dish. Anchovy broth is seasoned with *doenjang* (soybean paste) and cooked with daikon radish, tofu, chilis, Korean zucchini, and green onions. Add *chadolbagi* (beef brisket deckle) or clams for a hearty stew.

Side Dish

Banchan

Banchan, a side dish served with rice and soup, refers to all types of dishes that are pan-fried, stir-fried or braised and also stews, kimchi, seasoned vegetables, and hot pot dishes. For a typical Korean meal, you will find bowls of rice and soup and small dishes of various side dishes made fresh that day. The soup can be left out if the side dish is a form of stew or hot pot with soup.

Kimchi-jjigae (Kimchi Stew)
Sundubu-jjigae (Soft Bean Curd Stew)
Neobiani (Marinated Grilled Beef Slices)
Dubugui (Pan-fried Bean Curd)
Galbi-jjim (Braised Short Ribs)
Maeun Dak-jjim (Spicy Braised Chicken)
Godeungeo-jorim (Braised Mackerel)
Kimchi-jeon (Kimchi Pancake)
Modum-jeon (Assorted Savory Pancakes)
Bindaetteok (Mung Bean Pancake)
Haemul-pajeon (Seafood and Green Onion Pancake)
Tteokbokki (Spicy Stir-fried Rice Cakes)
Jeyuk-bokkeum (Spicy Stir-fried Pork)
Ttukbaegi-bulgogi (Hot Pot Bulgogi)
Oi-kimchi (Cucumber Kimchi)
Baechu-kimchi (Kimchi)
Kkakdugi (Diced Radish Kimchi)
Nabak-kimchi (Spicy Water Kimchi)
Samsaek-namul (Three Seasoned Vegetables)

Chapter 2
Side Dish
Banchan

Chapter 2
Side Dish
Banchan

김치찌개
Kimchi-jjigae
Kimchi Stew

"Well-aged" kimchi and pork are slowly cooked for this spicy stew. Add beef or seafood instead of pork for an interesting twist. Kimchi-*jjigae* is a popular Korean stew dish that is enjoyed all year round.

Ingredients 2 servings

| 300 g napa cabbage kimchi | 100 g pork belly | 100 g tofu | 10 cm green onion | 1 piece of kelp (5 cm x 10 cm) |

| 1 Tbsp cooking oil | 2 tsp sugar | 1 tsp minced garlic | 1 tsp soy sauce (*jip-ganjang*) | a small pinch of black pepper | 3 cups of water |

The stew tastes better if you use well-fermented kimchi. You can also add ham, canned tuna, mushrooms, onions, and green chili to the stew. Any pork meat is fine, but pork belly (preferably with the skin) is used most often to make kimchi-*jjigae*. For those who prefer meat with little fat, use blade shoulder that has the right ratio of fat and meat. Arm shoulder with little fat and chewy texture are recommended also.

blade shoulder   arm shoulder

What is *jjigae*?

There are more solid ingredients than liquid and the flavor is richer than *guk* (soup). The broth is seasoned with *gochujang*, *doenjang* or *jip-ganjang*.

Oi-gamjeong (Royal Court Gochujang Stew)

Royal court cuisine made with *gochujang*, cucumber, and beef

Chadolbagi Doenjang-jjigae (Beef Brisket Soybean Paste Stew)

Doenjang-jjigae with beef brisket deckle

Dongtae-jjigae (Pollack Stew)

Fish stew made with pollack, tofu, daikon radish, and *gochutgaru*, and seasoned with *jip-gangang*

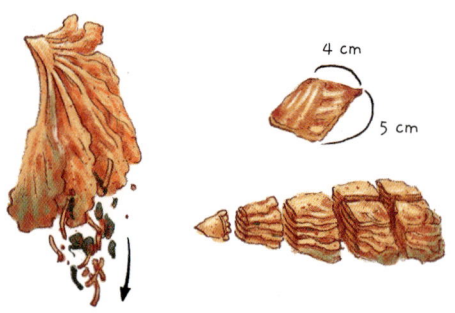

1 Remove part of the kimchi stuffing and cut into 4 cm x 5 cm pieces.

2 Cut pork into 3 cm x 4 cm pieces.

3 Boil kelp in 3 cups of water and pour over a colander to make broth.

4 Cut tofu into 2.5 cm x 3 cm x 1 cm pieces.

5 Thinly slice green onions diagonally.

6 Sauté pork with oil.

When the meat changes in color, add kimchi and continue to cook.

Add kelp broth and sugar, and keep cooking.

7 When the kimchi is softened, add tofu, green onions, and minced garlic and cook for 2 to 3 minutes.

Season with *jip-ganjang* and black pepper.

Let's make **budae-jjigae!**

Budae-jjigae (sausage stew) is made by adding sausages, canned ham, and other ingredients into kimchi-*jjigae*. It was first made after the Korean War using surplus processed meats from the U.S. military bases.

Kimchi, canned ham, sausage, tofu, and baked beans are cooked in kelp broth. Green onions, minced garlic, and *ssukgat* (crown daisy) are added in the end and seasoned with salt and black pepper. You can also add soybean sprouts, onions, mushrooms, ramen noodles, udon noodles, or rice cakes to the stew.

Grandma~ Could I have some ramen noodles in the stew?

Grandma~ I would like some rice cakes please!

Chapter 2
Side Dish
Banchan

순두부찌개
Sundubu-jjigae

Soft Bean Curd Stew

Sundubu or soft tofu is cooked with pork, beef or clams for this dish. Korea's tofu-making abilities go back hundreds of years, and people have enjoyed various tofu dishes prepared in different ways.

Ingredients 2 servings

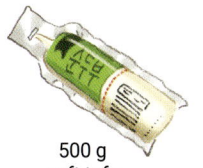   

| 500 g soft tofu | 50 g minced pork | 1 Tbsp cooking oil | a pinch of salt | 1 cup of water | 5 cm green onion |

seasoning

| 1 Tbsp soy sauce (*jip-ganjang*) | 1 Tbsp *gochutgaru* | 1 Tbsp sesame oil | 1 tsp minced green onion | 1 tsp minced garlic |

Tofu

Protein is extracted from soybean and hardened with magnesium chloride.

It is unknown when Korea first made tofu, but it is assumed that the skill was passed down from the Yuan Dynasty China at the end of the Goryeo Period in the 14th century.

Several varieties of tofu are available in Korea, including firm tofu for stew, extra firm tofu for pan frying, soft tofu, silken tofu, and fried tofu, *yubu*. (See p. 81.)

Honey! Can you teach me how to make *sundubu-jjigae*?

Sure! It's a good idea for you to learn how to make your favorite food. Let's start by buying the ingredients.

2 Slice green onions into 0.2 cm thick circles.

1 Cut the tube package in half and pour contents into a colander to drain.

1 T jip-ganjang 1 T gochutgaru 1 T sesame oil 1 t minced green onion 1 t minced garlic

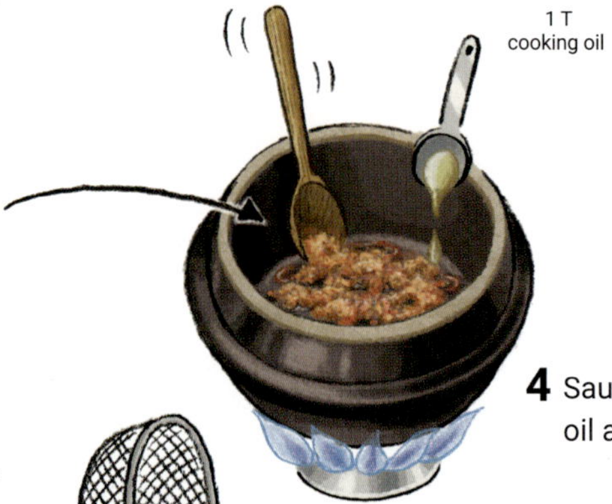

1 T cooking oil

3 Mix all the seasoning ingredients.

4 Sauté minced pork with oil and seasoning.

1 cup of water

5 Add water to boil.

Add soft tofu.

When the stew simmers, season with salt.

Garnish with sliced green onion and serve.

80

Different kinds of tofu available in Korean supermarkets

Look at all the tofu~ Now, where can I find sundubu?

Firm tofu for stew

Extra firm tofu for pan frying

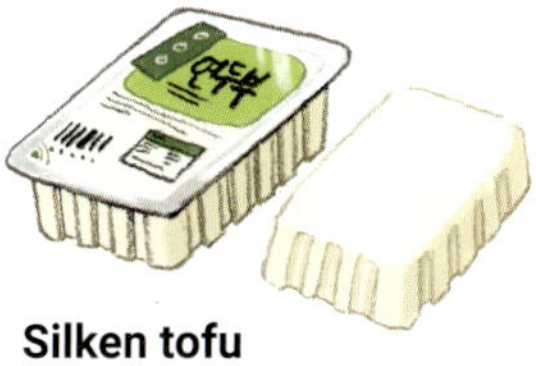

Silken tofu often served with sauce to pour over

Fried tofu (*yubu*) used for making *yubu* rice and udon

Soft tofu (*sundubu*)

Here! I'm here!

How to store leftover tofu

Tofu retains a lot of water and is prone to go bad quickly. It is best to cook the tofu right after purchase or refrigerate the leftover in a sealed container with water.

Honey! Do you like my sundubu-jjigae?

Mmmm~ Not bad for the first try. Looking forward to your next one!

Chapter 2
Side Dish
Banchan

너비아니
Neobiani

Marinated Grilled Beef Slices

Thin slices of marinated beef are grilled over gentle heat for this popular beef dish. The name came from royal court and aristocrats in old seoul "*neobut neobut*," which means a shaking motion of thin cloth. There is a similar dish called *maekjeok* (grilled seasoned meat slices) that was made since the Goguryeo period which is believed to be the origin of *neobiani*. It is a favorite meat dish among Koreans and foreigners alike.

Ingredients 2 servings

 300 g beef striploin

 1 tsp pine nuts

 a drizzle of cooking oil

---

marinade

 2 Tbsp soy sauce (*yangjo-ganjang*)

 1 Tbsp sugar

 1 Tbsp honey

 2 Tbsp minced green onion

 1 Tbsp minced garlic

 2 tsp sesame seeds

 a small pinch of black pepper

 2 tsp sesame oil

 2 Tbsp Asian pear juice

---

The beef striploin is for this dish. It is lean and tender, making it the most suitable for this marinated and grilled dish. Flavorful loin or lean tenderloin can also be used. Cut the beef against the grain to make it tender. Frozen meat must be thawed and the blood-soaked up with a paper towel before marinating. Sprinkle sugar or Asian pear juice over the tough meat to tenderize.

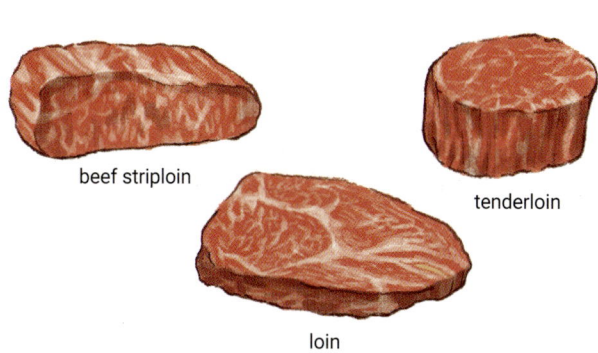

beef striploin

tenderloin

loin

seoksoe (gridiron)

sutbul (charcoal)

Start grilling from high heat and gradually turn down the heat to low as not to burn. Grilling directly over charcoal rather than using a frying pan will enhance the flavor.

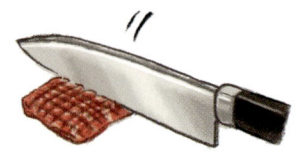

1 Blot the meat with a paper towel and cut it into 0.4 cm thick, 5 cm x 6 cm squares.

2 Make shallow cuts with a knife.

3 Peel the Asian pear, grate and squeeze in a cotton cooking cloth to make juice. (See p. 20.) When you don't have an Asian pear, sprinkle sugar on the meat and leave it for a while to make the meat tender.

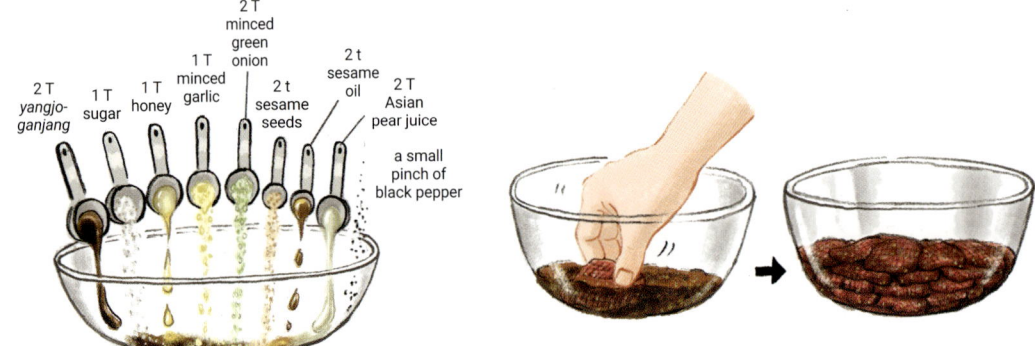

4 Make the marinade sauce.

5 Thoroughly coat beef with sauce and let sit.

or

6 Coat a frying pan or a gridiron with oil and lay beef side by side on the grill. You can also use an electric/gas grill.

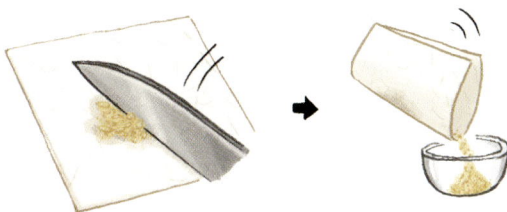

7 Mince pine nuts over *hanji* to make powder. (See p. 22.)

8 Serve grilled beef on a plate and garnish with pine nut powder. (Garnish can be left out.)

> **Neobiani** tastes almost the same as **bulgogi**. What is the difference between the two?

> Bulgogi is made with very thin slices of beef cut with a slicer, and *neobiani* is made with thicker beef.

> Oh, so the difference is the thickness.

> Grandma, then what is the difference between **steak** and **neobiani**?

> Steak and *neobiani* have different thicknesses. Also, the sauce is added to the steak after it is cooked whereas *neobiani* is seasoned before being grilled.

> The sauce ingredients are different. *Neobiani* uses soy sauce, sugar, green onions, garlic, sesame seeds, sesame oil, and black pepper. Steak uses flour, butter, onions, carrots, celery, tomatoes, laurel leaves, salt, pepper and so on. So the taste and flavor are different.

두부구이
Dubugui

Pan-fried Bean Curd

Bloted sliced tofu is pan-fried with oil and dipped in a soy sauce-based sauce. This easy-to-make dish is also high in vegetable protein.

Ingredients 2 servings

 1 tub of tofu (300 g)

 1/2 tsp salt

 1 Tbsp cooking oil

sauce

 2 Tbsp soy sauce (*yangjo-ganjang*)

 1 Tbsp vinegar

 1 tsp sugar

 1 tsp minced green onion

 1/2 tsp minced garlic

 1 tsp sesame oil

 a small pinch of *gochutgaru*

 a small pinch of sesame seeds

Make **dubujorim (braised tofu)** with pan-fried tofu!

Put pan-fried tofu in a pot and add the soy sauce-based sauce minus the vinegar on top of it. Add some water and cook for a few minutes with the lid closed. This is a popular *banchan*.

The tofu soaked the sauce, making it soft and moist. It goes well with a bowl of rice.

2/3 cup of water

1 Cut the tofu into 1 cm thick, 3 cm x 4 cm squares. Sprinkle with salt to draw out water and blot the water with a cotton cooking cloth.

2 In a pan with oil, pan-fry the tofu on both sides until golden brown. (Shake the pan gently to keep the tofu from sticking to the pan.)

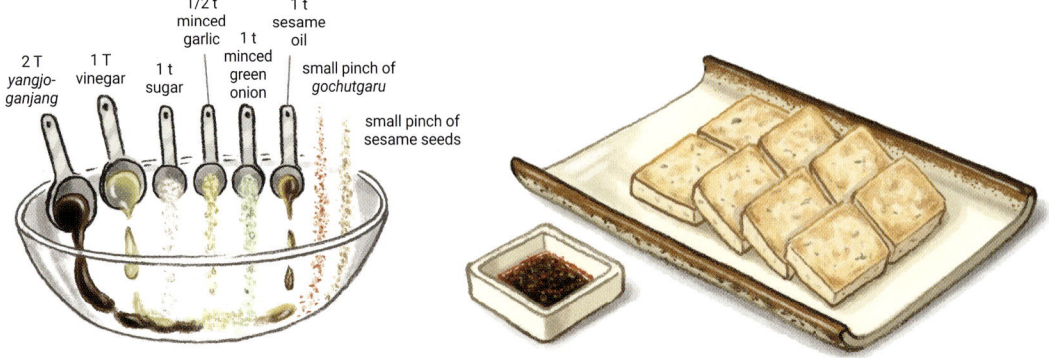

3 Mix the ingredients to make the sauce.

4 Serve the sauce on the side in a small bowl or drizzle over the tofu.

Making Tofu

Soak the soybeans (preferably recently harvested) for 7 to 8 hours and drain.

Grind the soaked soybeans with enough water.

Boil the soybean mixture in a large pot.

Pour the cooked soybean mixture to a cotton bag and squeeze well to extract the soy liquid.

Slowly boil the soy liquid in a large pot. Swirl with wooden paddle.

Add tofu clotting agent (magnesium chloride) and adjust the portion to make white curds.

Transfer the curds to a tofu mold lined with a cotton cooking cloth.

Cover the curds with the cloth and place a weight on top to begin pressing out the liquid.

Cut the firm tofu into small blocks.

Chapter 2
Side Dish
Banchan

갈비찜
Galbi-jjim

Braised Short Ribs

Beef ribs, usually made with Korean beef, or *Hanwoo*, are cut into small pieces, then marinated and braised. They are typically served on traditional holidays and special occasions. Short ribs from female veal are especially tender and tasty but pork ribs are also widely used. The slow-cooked meat falls easily from the bone, and the rich sauce should have a slightly bland and sweet flavor.

Ingredients 2 servings

 500 g beef ribs (5 cm pieces)
 5 g dried shiitake mushroom
 50 g carrot
 100 g onion
 2 eggs
 15 g water parsley (stem only)

 4 ginkgo nuts
 10 g dried jujube
 4 chestnuts
 1 tsp pine nuts
 1 Tbsp flour
 a drizzle of cooking oil
 2 cups of water

marinade

 4 Tbsp soy sauce (*yangjo-ganjang*)
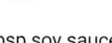
 3 Tbsp minced green onion
 1 1/2 Tbsp minced garlic
 2 Tbsp sugar
 1 Tbsp sesame oil
 1 Tbsp sesame seeds

 small pinch of black pepper
 1 tsp ginger juice
 4 Tbsp Asian pear juice

> Buy ribs that are cut into roughly 5 cm pieces. Onions help to remove the smell of fat and enhances the flavor, so add them from the beginning. You can also add daikon radish to the recipe.

You can make pork ribs instead of beef ribs. Add potatoes and red chilis. The recipe for making braised pork ribs is the same as braised beef ribs, but instead of adding water straight to the ribs, sauté the marinated ribs until brown before adding water.

Dwaeji Galbi-jjim
(Braised Pork Ribs)

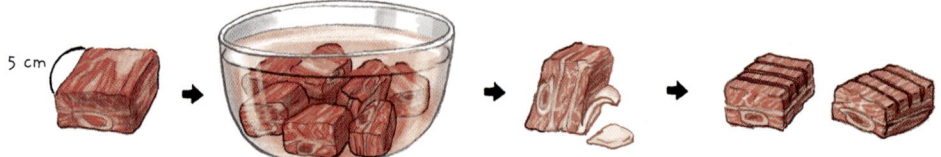

1 Soak meat in cold water for 30 minutes to draw out the blood. Drain, remove the fat and make shallow cuts.

2 Boil enough water to cover all the meat. Add meat, and when the water boils again drain it.

3 Peel ginger, grate, and squeeze in cotton cooking cloth to make ginger juice. Make Asian pear juice in the same method. (See p. 20.) Omit Asian pear if you don't have and add 1 tsp sugar instead.

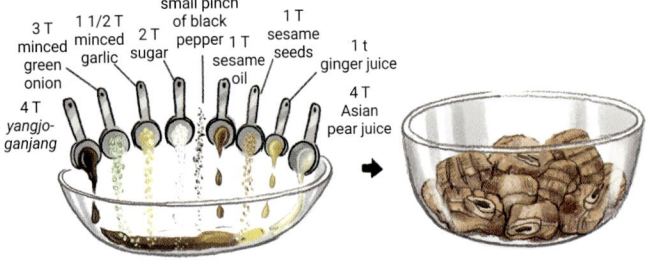

4 Make the marinade sauce.　　Thoroughly coat the ribs and leave for 10 minutes.

5 Wash shiitake mushroom and soak in water. Remove stem and divide into 3 or 4 sections.

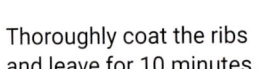
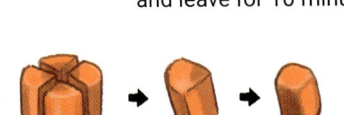

6 Peel carrots and cut into 4 cm pieces. Divide into quarters and round the edges.

7 Peel onions and divide into 4 sections.

8 Peel chestnuts.

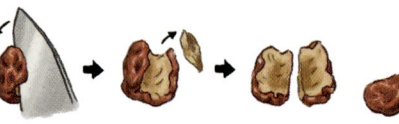

9 Remove the pit from dried jujube and cut in half.

10 Pan-fry ginkgo nuts with oil and rub with a paper towel to remove the skin.

11 Seperate egg white and yolk and make separate *jidan*. (See p. 21 for *jidan*.)

12 Skewer water parsley stems with wooden picks and coat with flour and beaten eggs. Pan fry with oil, remove picks and cut into a diamond shape. (See p. 155 step 7 for *minarichodae*.)

13 Add marinated ribs, onion and water to a thick pot, close lid, and boil in high heat.

Reduce to medium heat and cook for 20 minutes.

When the meat is cooked through, add chestnut, dried jujube, shiitake mushrooms, and carrots.

Spoon liquid over the ingredients and cook for 10 minutes in low heat.

Serve ribs and vegetables in a casserole dish, garnish with egg *jidan*, pan-fried water parsley (*minarichodae*), and pine nuts.

> Chapter 2
> Side Dish
> Banchan

매운닭찜
Maeun Dak-jjim

Spicy Braised Chicken

Cut the chicken into bite-size pieces, remove the fat, and add a spicy sauce made with *gochujang* and *gochutgaru*. Braise the chicken with vegetables, and you get a spicy dish. *Dakjjim* was originally made with a soy sauce-based sauce, but spicy ("*maeun*" in Korean) *dakjjim* has also become popular as people prefer hot taste.

Ingredients 3–4 servings

 1 whole chicken (800 g)

 1 red chili

 100 g carrot

 150 g potato

 100 g onion

1 green chili

 1 Tbsp cooking oil

 1 1/2 cups of water

---

marinade

 1 Tbsp *gochujang*

 2 Tbsp *gochutgaru*

 4 Tbsp soy sauce (*yangjo-ganjang*)

 3 Tbsp sugar

 1 Tbsp sesame oil

 4 Tbsp minced green onion

 2 Tbsp minced garlic

 2 tsp ginger juice

 1/2 tsp black pepper

> This is also known as *dakbokeumtang*, and it is especially popular among young people. Leave out the *gochujang* and *gochutgaru* and add 2 tsp of *yangjo-ganjang* to make a sweet and savory soy sauce-based *dakjjim*. Flat glass noodles go well with this dish. This soy sauce-braised chicken is also called *jjimdak*.

Jjimdak

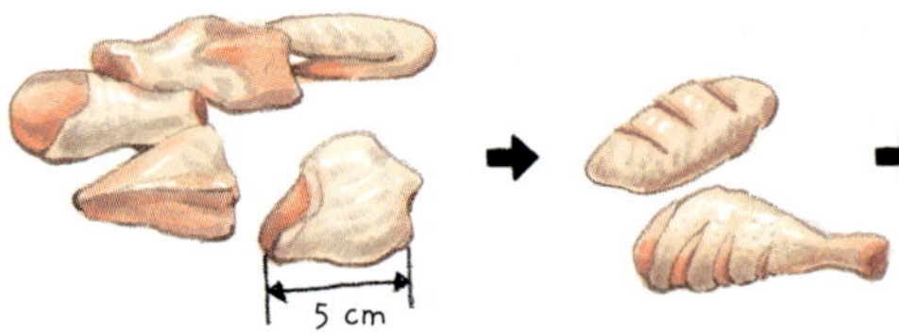

1 Cut chicken into 5 cm pieces and make shallow cuts with a knife. Parboil and rinse in cold water to remove fat.

Marinade sauce ingredients:
- 1 T gochujang
- 2 T gochutgaru
- 4 T yangjo-ganjang
- 4 T minced green onion
- 2 T minced garlic
- 3 T sugar
- 1 T sesame oil
- 2 t ginger juice
- 1/2 t black pepper

1/2 of sauce

2 Make the marinade sauce.

Marinate prepared chicken with half the sauce.

3 Slice red and green chilis diagonally and remove seeds.

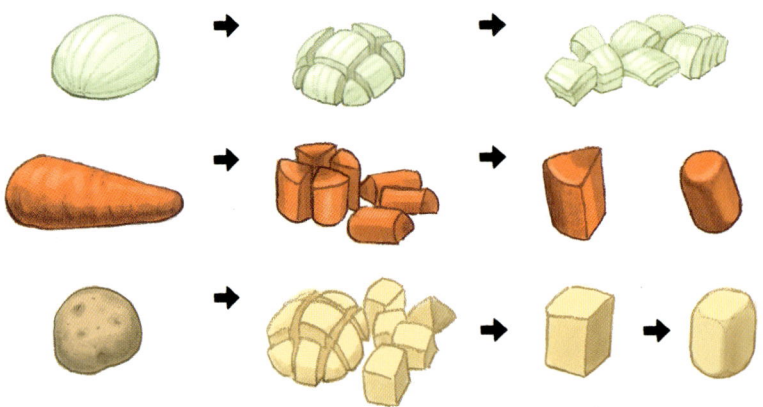

4 Cut onions, carrots, and potatoes in large bite-size pieces and round the edges of the carrots and potatoes.

5 Sauté chicken lightly with oil.

Add water, close lid, and cook for 10 minutes in medium heat.

6 When the chicken is half cooked, add sauce and vegetables.

Close lid and cook for 10 minutes.

Open the lid and braise in low heat until there is little liquid left in the pot.

Set aside a small amount of *dakjjim* liquid and fry it with rice, toasted laver flakes, sesame oil, green onions, and kimchi directly in the pot to make delicious fried rice. Scorched rice called *nooroongji* stuck to the bottom of the pot is also a tasty treat.

Chapter 2
Side Dish
Banchan

고등어조림
Godeungeo-jorim
Braised Mackerel

The affordable and widely-available mackerel is a popular fish in Korea that is usually grilled or braised. Mackerel and daikon radish are braised in kelp broth and spicy sauce in a pot for this dish. This braising method can be used for cooking any type of fish at home as well as restaurants.

Ingredients 2 servings

 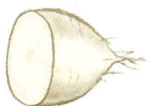   

| 1 fresh mackerel (500 g) | 300 g daikon radish | 1 red chili | 1 green chili | 10 cm green onion |

marinade

   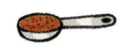 

| 1 Tbsp soy sauce (*jip-ganjang*) | 2 Tbsp soy sauce (*yangjo-ganjang*) | 1 Tbsp sesame oil | 1 Tbsp *gochutgaru* | 1 Tbsp *gochujang* |

| 2 Tbsp clear rice wine | 1 Tbsp minced garlic | 1 Tbsp sugar | 1 tsp minced ginger | 1 tsp sesame seeds |

broth

| 2 cups of water | 1 piece of kelp (5 cm x 10 cm) |

You can braise hairtail, Spanish mackerel, or saury in the same method. Substitute daikon radish for potatoes. For those who don't like spicy food, add a little bit more soy sauce instead of *gochujang* and *gochutgaru* to make soy sauced-braised mackerel.
Grilling mackerel preserved in salt is another way to enjoy this fish. See how you can prepare mackerel for grilling on the next page.

Godeungeo-gui
(Grilled Mackerel)

Godeungeo*-kimchi *Jorim
(Braised Kimchi Mackerel)

Lay kimchi instead of daikon radish under the mackerel and add kelp broth to make braised kimchi mackerel.

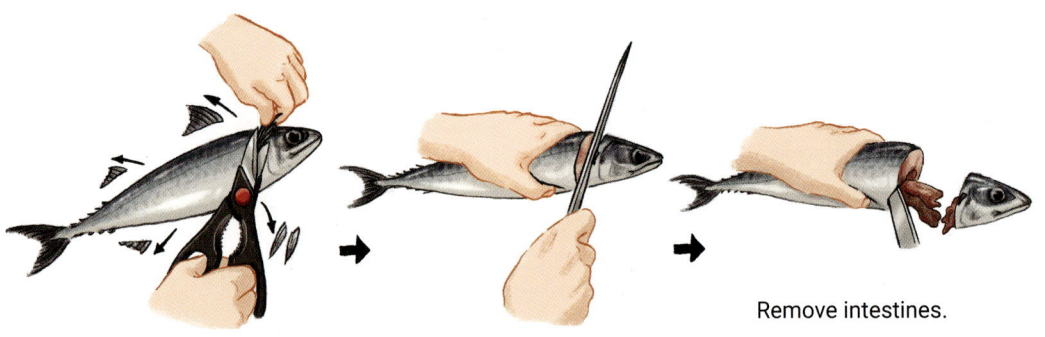

Remove intestines.

1 Snip the fins off using kitchen scissors.

Cut off the head.

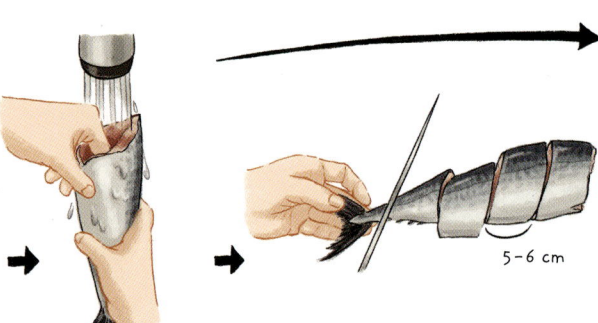

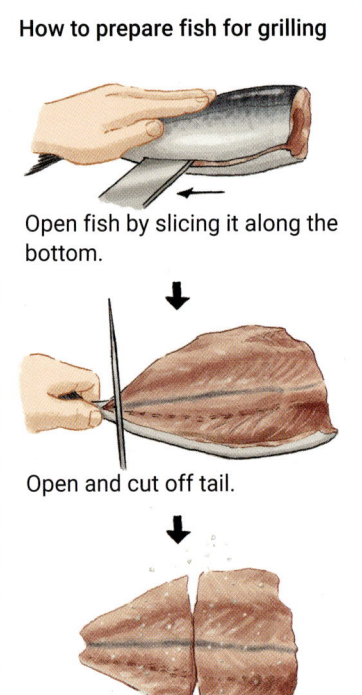

How to prepare fish for grilling

Open fish by slicing it along the bottom.

Open and cut off tail.

Cut into the size for use and season with salt.

Clean thoroughly with water.

Divide into 5 cm to 6 cm pieces and remove the tail.

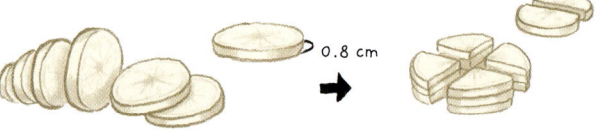

2 Slice the radish into 0.8 cm pieces and cut into four. Cut in half if radish is small.

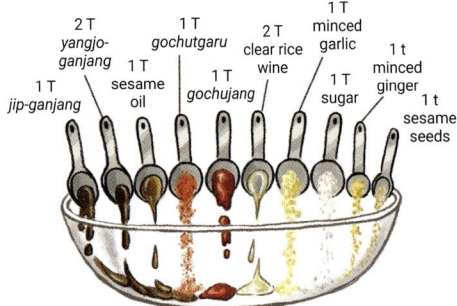

2 T yangjo-ganjang
1 T gochutgaru
2 T clear rice wine
1 T minced garlic
1 t minced ginger
1 T sesame oil
1 T gochujang
1 T sugar
1 t sesame seeds
1 T jip-ganjang

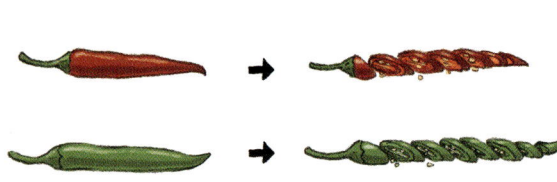

3 Mix sauce ingredients.

4 Slice green and red chilis diagonally.

5 Slice green onion diagonally.

6 Spread radish onto the bottom of a thick pan. Add water and kelp and boil.

Turn off the heat and remove kelp.

Add mackerel and sauce.

Open lid partially and cook in high heat. When the broth boils, cook for 10 minutes on medium heat.

Add green and red chilis and green onions.

Keep the lid opened and braise for 10 more minutes, pouring broth over fish continuously.

> Chapter 2
> **Side Dish**
> Banchan

김치전
Kimchi-jeon

Kimchi Pancake

Chopped kimchi, green chilis, and sliced onions are added to a flour batter and pan-fried for this dish. Kimchi is a staple side dish for *bansangcharim* but it can also be used as an ingredient for various dishes such as kimchi soup, kimchi pancake, and kimchi fried rice.

Ingredients 2 X 20 cm in diameter

| 100 g kimchi | 1 cup of flour | 100 g minced pork | 1/2 onion | 2 green chilis |

| 1 egg | 1 cup of water | 1/2 tsp salt | 3 Tbsp cooking oil |

dipping sauce (soy-vinegar)

| 4 Tbsp soy sauce (*yangjo-ganjang*) | 2 Tbsp vinegar | small pinch of sugar | 1 Tbsp water |

Let's make **kimchi-*bokkeumbap*** (kimchi fried rice)!

Stir-fry minced kimchi, pork, and onions in a pan with oil and add rice. Season with salt and pepper and finish with a small drizzle of sesame oil. The result is a spicy and savory kimchi-*bokkeumbap* (kimchi fried rice) that is a favorite for many Koreans.

The grain, animal protein, vegetables, and fermented kimchi in this dish make a nutritionally well-balanced meal. You can also add Korean zucchini, carrots, mushrooms, beef, or ham.

1 Chop the kimchi into small pieces.

2 Julienne the onion and dice the green chilis.

3 Mix kimchi, onion, green chilis, and pork with flour, egg, salt, and water.

4 Coat frying pan with enough oil and ladle the batter into the pan. Flatten the batter and cook on both sides.

You can fry into smaller portions.

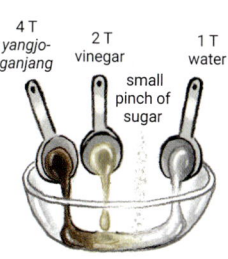

5 Cut the pancake into small pieces.

6 Make the soy-vinegar dipping sauce.

7 Serve the pancake on a plate with the sauce.

Let's make **kimchi-*jeok*** with an interesting kimchi texture.

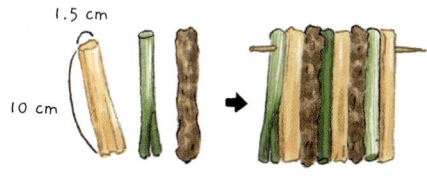

Squeeze the juice from the kimchi and cut into 1.5 cm wide, 10 cm long strips. Cut the beef in the same size as the kimchi, marinate it and pan-fry. Cut the green onion in the same length. Skewer the ingredients in order.

Coat with flour and dip in beaten eggs.

Coat frying pan with enough oil and pan-fry the skewers on both sides. Remove the picks and serve.

Chapter 2
Side Dish
Banchan

Modum-jeon
모둠전

Assorted Savory Pancakes

Meat, seafood, and vegetables are prepared into thin slices or small portions and coated with flour and eggs and pan-fried in oil. It is always made on special occasions such as celebrations and holidays.

Ingredients 4 servings

Korean zucchini *jeon* (*aehobakjeon*)

| 1 Korean zucchini | 1/3 cup of flour | 2 eggs | small pinch of salt | a drizzle of cooking oil |

fish *jeon* (*saengseonjeon*)

| 200 g cod fillet | 1/3 cup of flour | 2 eggs | small pinch of salt | small pinch of black pepper | a drizzle of cooking oil |

beef *jeon* (*yukwonjeon*)

| 200 g minced beef | 50 g tofu | 1/3 cup of flour | 2 eggs | a drizzle of cooking oil |

| 1 tsp salt | 1 tsp sesame oil | 1 Tbsp minced green onion | 1 tsp minced garlic | small pinch of black pepper |

dipping sauce (soy-vinegar)

| 4 Tbsp soy sauce (*yangjo-ganjang*) | 2 Tbsp vinegar | 1 Tbsp water | small pinch of sugar |

Jeon and Jeok

Jeon: The ingredient is thinly sliced and coated with flour and eggs and pan-fried. Various ingredients such as white fish fillet, green chilis, shiitake mushroom, sweet potato, daikon radish, and napa cabbage are used to make *jeon*.

Jeok: Sliced ingredients are skewered and pan-fried.

San-jeok
Raw ingredients cut into same length, seasoned, skewered and pan-fried.

tteok-sanjeok

Jijimnureum-jeok
Cooked ingredients are skewered and coated with flour and eggs before being pan-fried.

jijimnureum-jeok

Nureum-jeok
Cooked ingredients are skewered with wooden picks.

hwayangjeok

Korean Zucchini Jeon (Aehobakjeon)

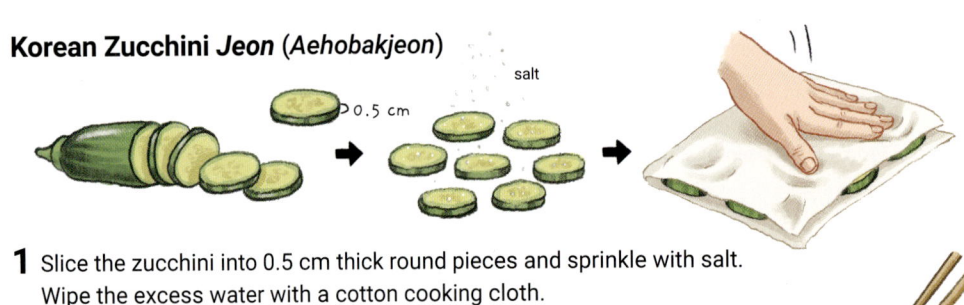

1 Slice the zucchini into 0.5 cm thick round pieces and sprinkle with salt. Wipe the excess water with a cotton cooking cloth.

2 Beat the eggs.

3 Coat the sliced zucchini with flour and dip it in the eggs.

4 Coat the pan with enough oil and pan-fry the zucchini on both sides.

Fish Jeon (Saengseonjeon)

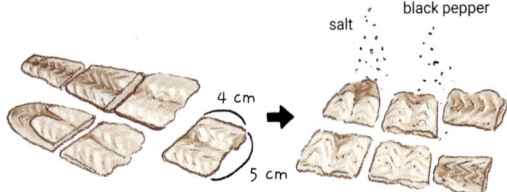

1 Cut the fish fillet into 4 cm x 5 cm pieces and season with salt and pepper.

2 When the salt is melted, wipe the excess water with a cotton cooking cloth.

3 Beat the eggs.

4 Coat the fish with flour and dip it in the eggs.

5 Coat the pan with enough oil and pan-fry the fish on both sides.

Beef *Jeon* (*Yukwonjeon*)

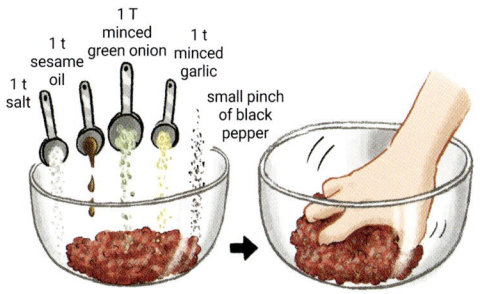

1 Season the minced beef and mix with hands.

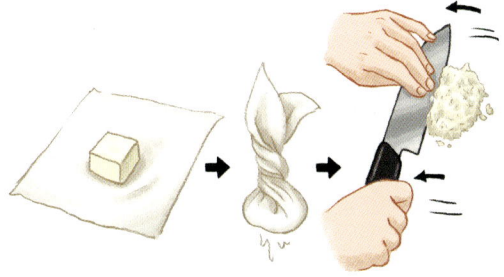

2 Squeeze out the water from the tofu in a cotton cooking cloth and mash with a knife blade.

3 Mix the beef with tofu and shape into 1 cm thick, 3 cm to 5 cm wide flat circles.

4 Beat the eggs.

5 Coat the patties with flour and dip it in the eggs.

6 Coat the pan with enough oil and pan-fry on both sides.

7 Make the soy-vinegar dipping sauce.

Place all three *jeon* in one plate.
Serve with soy-vinegar dipping sauce.

Chapter 2
Side Dish
Banchan

빈대떡
Bindaetteok

Mung Bean Pancake

Ground mung beans are pan-fried with a lot of oil to make this savory pancake dish. In the old days, mung bean pancakes were made like rice cakes with sweet red bean paste and chestnuts. But now, it is a savory pancake made with pork, beef, kimchi, mung bean sprouts, and mushroom. This is an all-time favorite *anju* (food consumed with alcohol) that goes well with *makgeolli* (Korean rice wine).

Ingredients 2 servings

| 2 cups of peeled mung bean | 1 cup of water | 1/2 tsp salt | a pinch of black pepper | 5 cm green onion |

| 100 g minced beef | 100 g napa cabbage kimchi | 100 g mung bean sprouts | 50 g oyster mushroom | drizzle of cooking oil |

beef marinade

| 1 tsp soy sauce (*yangjo-ganjang*) | 1 Tbsp minced green onion | 1 tsp minced garlic | 1 tsp sesame oil | a pinch of sesame seeds | a pinch of black pepper |

dipping sauce (soy-vinegar)

| 4 Tbsp soy sauce (*yangjo-ganjang*) | 1 Tbsp water | 2 Tbsp vinegar | 1 tsp *gochutgaru* | small pinch of sugar |

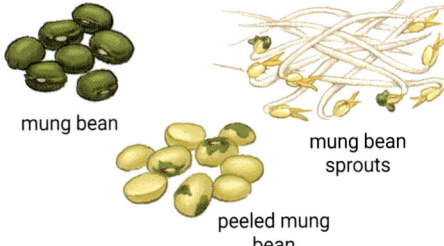

mung bean

mung bean sprouts

peeled mung bean

Nokdu (Mung Bean)

Since the past, mung bean is known as a natural antidote that emits toxic substances from the body and it is a quality food that helps metabolism. It is a widely used ingredient to make *bindaetteok* (mung bean pancake), *cheongpomuk* (mung bean jelly), rice cake topping and mung bean tea. The beans are grown into mung bean sprouts which is also a popular vegetable.

History of *Bindaetteok*

During the Joseon period, a group of wandering people, who left their homes after a bad year of harvest, gathered outside Namdaemun Gate in Seoul. Rich people from the city made mung bean pancakes and offered to these people. This food became known as *binjatteok*, *binja* meaning "the poor." It is now called *bindaetteok*, and it is made as a savory pancake with meat and vegetables, not as a sweet dish like the old days.

Binjatteok (*Bingja*)

2 cups of peeled mung bean

1 cup of water

1 Soak the mung beans in water for more than 3 hours and wash as you remove the remaining skin.

Drain the beans and grind in a blender with 1 cup of water.

1 t yangjo-ganjang, 1 T minced green onion, 1 t minced garlic, 1 t sesame oil, a pinch of sesame seeds, a pinch of black pepper

2 Season the minced beef.

3 Thinly slice the kimchi.

4 Dice the green onion.

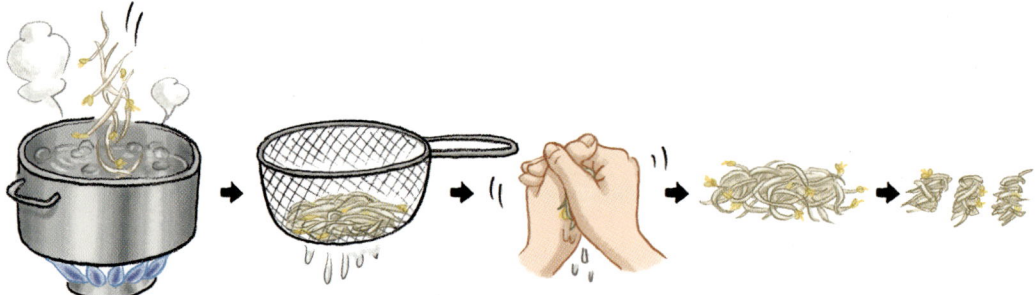

5 Blanch the mung bean sprouts, squeeze out the water and dice into small pieces.

6 Blanch the oyster mushroom, squeeze out the water and dice into small pieces.

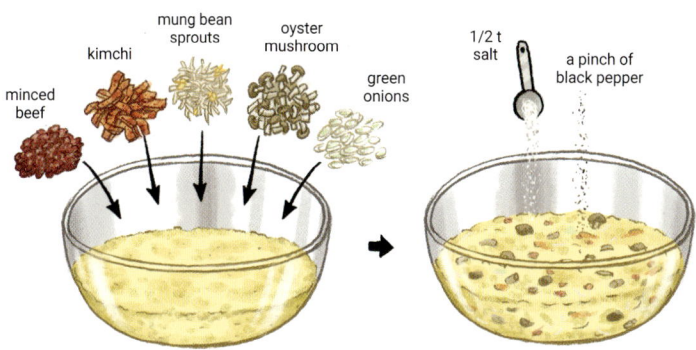

7 Add beef, kimchi, mung bean sprouts, oyster mushroom, and green onions to the ground mung bean and season with salt and pepper.

9 Make the soy-vinegar dipping sauce.

8 In a pan coated with oil, ladle one scoop of the batter to make 7 cm to 8 cm pancakes. Cook golden brown on both sides.

10 Serve warm with the dipping sauce.

Makgeolli, the Perfect Drink with *Jeon*

Steamed rice is mixed with *nuruk* (traditional fermentation starter) and water. When fermented, filter for this traditional rice wine. The rice is dissolved in the fermentation process, resulting in a milky appearance.

It is called *takju* for its opaque color, *tak* means "turbid." Also it is called *makgeolli* for filtering roughly through a cotton cooking cloth, *mak* means "in unorderly fashion."

Chapter 2
Side Dish
Banchan

해물파전
Haemul-pajeon
Seafood and Green Onion Pancake

Jjokpa (small green onion) or *silpa* (thread green onion) are topped with various seafood and pan-fried in oil for this dish. The flavor of green onion goes well with the seafood. You can use any seafood you like such as squid, oyster, clam meat or shrimp depending on preferences.

Ingredients 2 X 20 cm in diameter

200 g thread green onion (*silpa*)	50 g squid	30 g oyster (or clam meat)	20 g shrimps	50 g beef	a drizzle of cooking oil

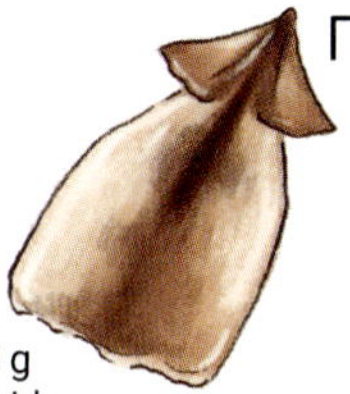

you can also use frozen processed seafood

batter

1 1/2 cups of flour	1 1/2 cups of water	1 egg	1 tsp salt

beef marinade

1 tsp soy sauce (*yangjo-ganjang*)	1 tsp sugar	1 tsp minced green onion	1 tsp minced garlic	small pinch of black pepper	a drizzle of sesame oil	small pinch of sesame seeds

dipping sauce (soy-vinegar)

4 Tbsp soy sauce (*yangjo-ganjang*)	1 Tbsp water	2 Tbsp vinegar	1 tsp *gochutgaru*	small pinch of sugar

Leave out the seafood to make regular *pajeon* (green onion pancake). You can use any type of green onions to make it. *Jjokpa* or *silpa* are also used to make *pa*-kimchi (green onion kimchi) or *paganghoe* (blanched green onion wrap).

paganghoe

Koreans traditionally boiled the roots of green onions and drank the water to treat colds, coughs and sleeplessness. Green onions and garlic are widely used as seasoning because of the unique flavor and aroma that helps to get rid of the raw smell of meat and fish.

Different types of green onions

Daepa (Green Onion)
The stem is long and thick.

Jjokpa (Small Green Onion)
The top head is round and short.

Silpa (Thread Green Onion)
The stem is thin and short.

1 Remove the root part and wilted ends of green onions and wash. Cut into 20 cm length.

2 Thinly slice the beef and marinate it.

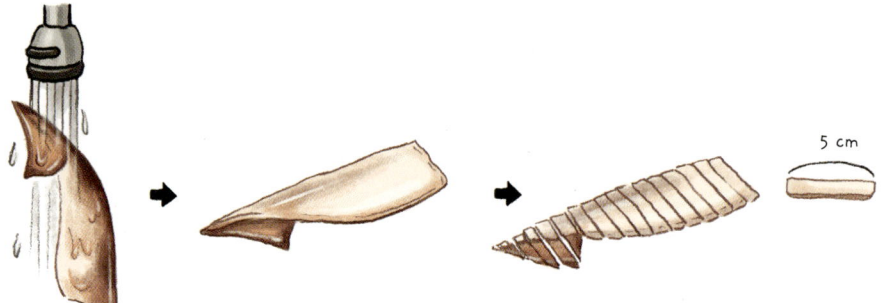

3 Wash the squid and cut into 5 cm long.

Wash the shrimp and oyster in salt water and drain.

4 Mix flour, egg, salt, and water to make the batter.

5 Put enough oil on a frying pan.

Ladle a scoop of batter into the pan and arrange green onions, seafood, and beef on top. Add little bit of batter over them.

Turn the pancake over to cook on both sides until golden brown.

Cut into bite-size pieces.

6 Make the soy-vinegar dipping sauce.

7 Serve with the dipping sauce.

> Chapter 2
> **Side Dish**
> Banchan

떡볶이
Tteokbokki

Spicy Stir-fried Rice Cakes

Cylinder-shaped white rice cakes are stir-fried with fish cakes, vegetables, and *gochujang* sauce. The spicy and slightly sweet red sauce goes well with the chewiness of the rice cakes and the flavor of the fish cakes.

Ingredients *2 servings*

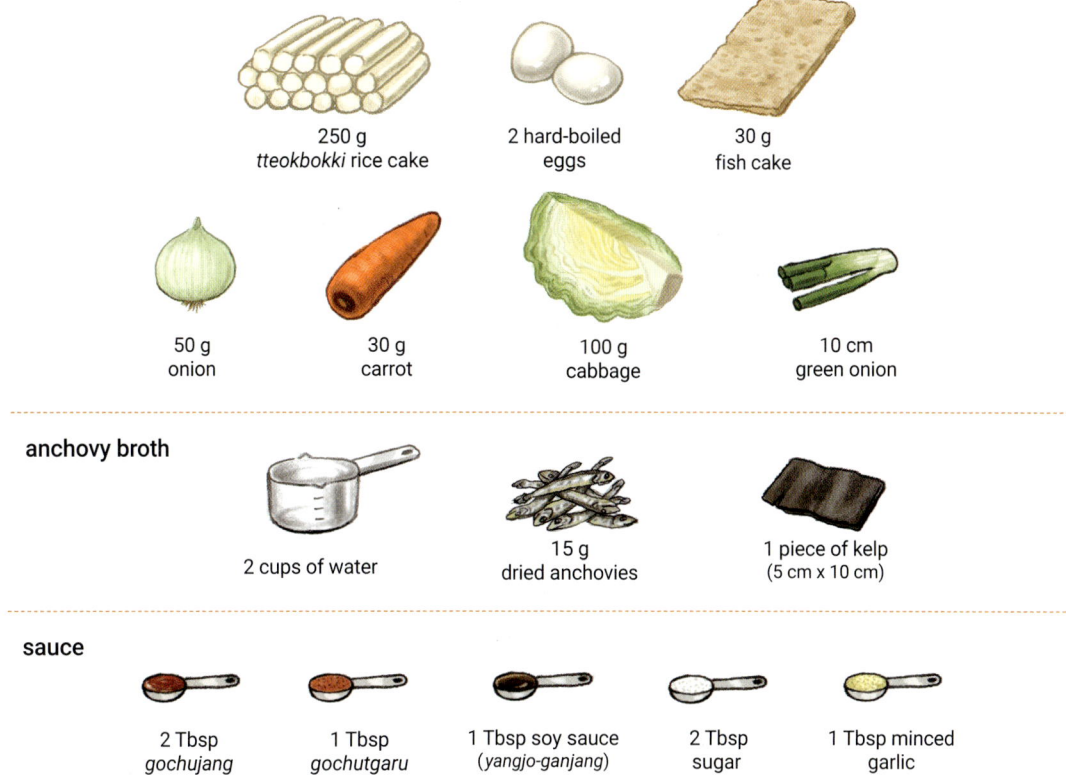

- 250 g *tteokbokki* rice cake
- 2 hard-boiled eggs
- 30 g fish cake
- 50 g onion
- 30 g carrot
- 100 g cabbage
- 10 cm green onion

anchovy broth
- 2 cups of water
- 15 g dried anchovies
- 1 piece of kelp (5 cm x 10 cm)

sauce
- 2 Tbsp *gochujang*
- 1 Tbsp *gochutgaru*
- 1 Tbsp soy sauce (*yangjo-ganjang*)
- 2 Tbsp sugar
- 1 Tbsp minced garlic

History of *Tteokbokki*

Gungjung-tteokbokki (soy sauce *tteokbokki*) was the original. It is unknown when spicy *gochujang tteokbokki* was first developed. Experts believe *gochujang tteokbokki* first became known in the late 1950s. Other ingredients like boiled eggs and ramen noodles are added to the spicy *tteokbokki*.

In some restaurants, *tteokbokki* is cooked and served right at the customer's table. The most popular place to go for these restaurants is the Sindangdong Tteokbokki Street in Seoul.

Tteokbokki **cooked on the table**

1 Remove the head and intestines of the anchovies.

2 Boil anchovies and kelp for 5 minutes and pour through a colander to make the broth.

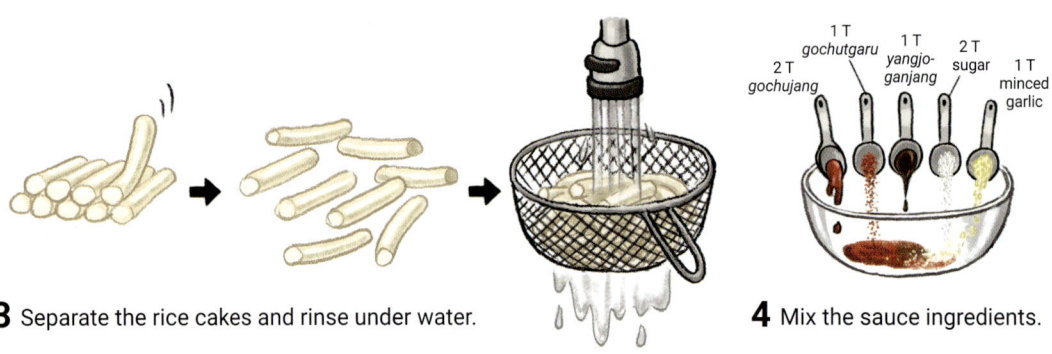

3 Separate the rice cakes and rinse under water.

4 Mix the sauce ingredients.

5 Cut the fish cakes into 2 cm x 4 cm pieces.

Slice cabbage into thick strips.

Julienne the onion.

6 Cut the carrot into 1 cm x 4 cm flat sticks.

Slice the green onion diagonally.

7 Lay the sliced cabbage and onion on a wide bottom pan.

Arrange the rice cakes, fish cakes, boiled eggs, carrot and green onions.

Pour the sauce and anchovy broth over the ingredients.

Cook in high heat.

Lower the heat when the sauce simmers. Cook until the rice cakes are soft and pouring sauce over occasionally.

Tteokbokki is a widely popular dish usually enjoyed from *pojangmacha* (street vendors) or *bunsikjip* (snack bars). *Oemuk* (fish cake skewer), *twigim* (deep-fried food), *sundae* (traditional sausage), *ggoma* gimbap (mini gimbap) are other popular snack foods enjoyed with *tteokbokki*.

sundae *twigim* *tteokbokki* *oemuk*

ggoma gimbap

Chapter 2
Side Dish
Banchan

제육볶음
Jeyuk-bokkeum

Spicy Stir-fried Pork

Sliced pork is marinated in *gochujang*, soy sauce, *gochutgaru*, and all the other ingredient and stir-fried with assorted vegetables. It is a popular Korean pork dish.

Ingredients 2 servings

| 250 g sliced pork for grilling | 50 g onion | 30 g carrot | 5 cm green onion | 1/3 *cheongyang*-chili | 1 Tbsp cooking oil |

---

marinade

| 1 Tbsp *gochujang* | 2 tsp *gochutgaru* | 1 Tbsp soy sauce (*yangjo-ganjang*) | 2 tsp sugar | 2 tsp starch syrup |

| 2 tsp minced garlic | 1/2 tsp ginger juice | 1/4 tsp black pepper | 1 tsp sesame seeds | 1 tsp sesame oil |

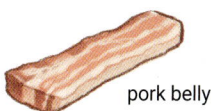

pork belly

You can make this dish with any pork cut, but use fatty pork belly for oily meaty taste or leg for light and lean depends on what you prefer.

leg

Preferably buy fresh pork instead of frozen, and if using frozen pork, slowly thaw it in the refrigerator before cooking.

You can add cabbage, Korean zucchini, and mushrooms. They go well with this dish.

Reduce the portion of meat and add more vegetables for less calories.

1 Cut pork into 5 cm to 6 cm pieces.

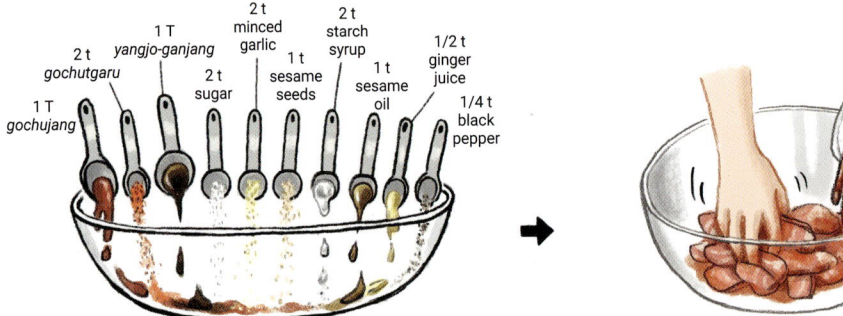

2 Mix ingredients for the marinade.

3 Marinate pork and set aside.

4 Julienne onions and slice green onions diagonally.

Thinly slice carrots, and chop cheongyang-chilis into small pieces.

5 Preheat frying pan with oil and pan-fry pork.

When the meat is cooked, add carrots, onions, chilis and green onions, and fry lightly.

Instead of *gochujang* and *gochutgaru*, add 2 Tbsp *yangjo-ganjang* to make a **soy sauce flavored *jeyuk-bokkeum*.**

Jeyuk-deopbap
Add *jeyuk-bokkeum* on top of rice to make spicy pork rice bowl.

Kimchi *Jeyuk-bokkeum*
Pan fry 5 cm to 6 cm sliced pork and kimchi. It is a simple dish you can make with kimchi at home, and it goes well with blanched tofu slices.

Osam-bulgogi
Pan fry squid and pork belly using the same recipe to make this dish.

Chapter 2
Side Dish
Banchan

뚝배기불고기
Ttukbaegi-bulgogi

Hot Pot Bulgogi

Marinated bulgogi is boiled with water in a *ttukbaegi* (clay pot). The meat is tender and the soup-like liquid is savory from the sauce and meat. *Ttukbaegi* is a Korean earthenware that can be used to cook over a direct flame. The pot retains heat for a long time and keeps the food warm during the entire meal. Unlike a casserole you share with others, this one-person dish is easy to make for one person.

Ingredients 2 servings

250 g
thinly sliced beef

50 g
onion

30 g
carrot

30 g
enoki mushroom

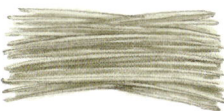
10 g
glass noodles

2 stems of
crown daisies

1 cup of water

1 piece of kelp
(5 cm x 5 cm)

---

beef marinade

1 1/2 Tbsp soy sauce
(*yangjo-ganjang*)

1 Tbsp
sugar

1 tsp
sesame oil

1 Tbsp minced
green onion

2 tsp minced
garlic

1 tsp sesame
seeds

1/4 tsp
black pepper

Bulgogi is a thinly sliced beef dish marinated with *neobiani* sauce and either grilled or stir-fried. It is a relatively modern dish that became popular when slicing tools became available for cutting thin slices of meat. The word "bulgogi" appears to be a new word, and it was documented as "*neobiani*" up until the 1950s.

Stir-frying in a frying pan is the most popular cooking method, but it can also be boiled in a clay pot, cooked in bulgogi pan with broth, or grilled on a grate. Add the cooked bulgogi liquid to rice for a tasty meal.

It is the most well-known Korean beef dish and a favorite among Koreans and non-Koreans.

1 Boil kelp in 1 cup of water. Remove kelp and set aside the broth.

2 Cook glass noodles in boiling water and rinse in cold water.

3 Mix ingredients to make the marinade.

4 Cut the thinly sliced beef to 5 cm pieces and marinate.

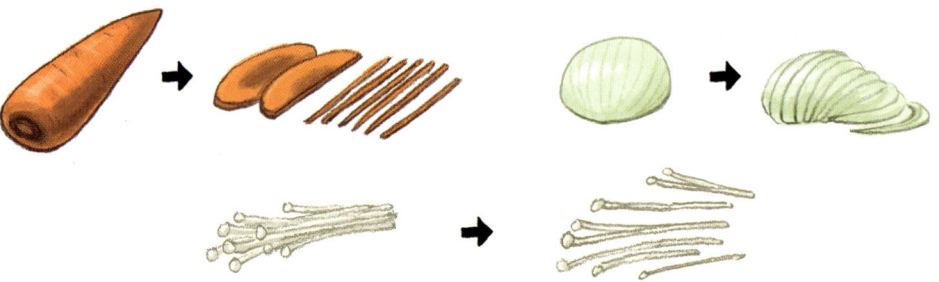

5 Thinly julienne carrots and onions, then pull apart enoki mushroom into smaller strands.

6 Sauté beef in *ttukbaegi*.

Add kelp broth from step 1 and stir well.

1 cup of kelp broth

Add carrots, onions, glass noodles, and enoki mushrooms.

Lastly, arrange crown daisies on top.

Cooking tools for making bulgogi

seoksoe (grill)

shallow pan or frying pan

bulgogi pan

ttukbaegi

Chapter 2
Side Dish
Banchan

오이김치
Oi-kimchi

Cucumber Kimchi

Cut the cucumber into 3 cm sections, cut into quarters halfway, and brine. Stuff with a seasoning made with salted shrimp, Korean chive, garlic, *gochutgaru*, sugar, and salt to make cucumber kimchi. It is the quickest and easiest types of kimchi to make. Reduce the amount of *gochutgaru* if you don't like spicy food, and you can still get that refreshing crunchy kimchi.

Ingredients about 800 g of *oi*-kimch

4 cucumbers   1 Tbsp salt

seasoning

50 g Korean chive

2 Tbsp minced garlic

2 Tbsp *gochutgaru*

1 Tbsp salted shrimp (*saeujeot*)

1 tsp sugar

1 tsp minced ginger

1 tsp salt

Different types of *oi*-kimchi

Oi-songsongi or *Oi-kkakdugi*
(Diced Cucumber Kimchi)

Cucumbers are diced into small cubes to make this kimchi. *Kkakdugi* was called "*songsongi*" in the Joseon court and it was brined and mixed with daikon radishes cut into the same size.

Oi-sobagi
(Stuffed Cucumber Kimchi)

Thick cucumbers are cut into 5 cm sections and cut with long slits lengthwise to create four cucumber spears that are held together at both ends. The sections are brined and stuffed with a spicy Korean chive sauce.

Saeujeot (Salted Shrimp)

Small shrimp are salted and fermented to make this condiment. There are several types of *saeujeot*, and what is made depends on the time of year the shrimp are harvested.

There is *ojeot* (May), *yukjeot* (June), *chujeot* (fall) and *dongbaekhajeot* (winter). *Yukjeot* is best for making *kimjang* and *ojeot* and *chujeok* are used for making side dishes.

Saeujeot is often used as a salty condiment for seasoning kimchi and stews and as a dipping sauce for boiled pressed pork.

1 Rub the cucumber with salt to wash and cut into 3 cm sections and divide into quarters. Divide into 6 pieces if the cucumber is very thick.

2 Sprinkle with salt and leave for 30 minutes. Transfer to a colander to drain excess water.

3 Dice Korean chive into 0.5 cm pieces and mince the salted shrimp.

4 Mix diced Korean chives, garlic, *gochutgaru*, ginger, salted shrimp, sugar, and salt to make the seasoning.

5 Season the cucumber from step 2. You can eat this right away like a salad or store it for a few days to enjoy different fermented flavor for each day. (*Oi*-kimchi can go soggy over the time, so it's best to eat it within a short time. Make sure the cucumbers are submerged in kimchi liquid to last longer.)

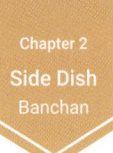

Chapter 2
Side Dish
Banchan

배추김치
Baechu-kimchi

Kimchi

This iconic fermented side dish is made with brined napa cabbage that is seasoned with *gochutgaru*, green onions, garlic, ginger, and salted seafood. It is a staple side dish that is always served at Korean meals. Napa cabbage kimchi is simply referred to as "kimchi" in Korea.

Ingredients about 2.5 kg of *baechu*-kimchi

- 1 head of napa cabbage (2 kg)
- 1 1/2 cups of salt
- 2 L water
- 300 g daikon radish
- 50 g small green onion (*jjokpa*)
- 50 g mustard leaf
- 50 g water parsley
- 2 Tbsp *gochutgaru*

seasoning
- 1/4 cup of salted shrimp (*saeujeot*)
- 1/2 cup of *gochutgaru*
- 2 Tbsp anchovy fish sauce
- 2 tsp sugar
- 1 whole head of garlic
- 20 g ginger

Kimjang Culture

A Korean table is never complete without a plate of kimchi. Koreans make large portions of kimchi to last the winter and the act of making and sharing kimchi is called *kimjang*. Eating kimchi was a way to supplement the body with nutrients that are lacking in the winter months. *Kimjang* is an annual event for many Korean households. *Jeotgal* (fermented seafood) is prepared in the spring, sea salt is bought in the summer, *gochutgaru* is made in late summer and kimchi is made from late fall to early winter. Villagers and family members got together to make kimchi as a group and shared what they made. *Kimjang* was added to UNESCO's Representative List of the Intangible Cultural Heritage of Humanity in 2013.

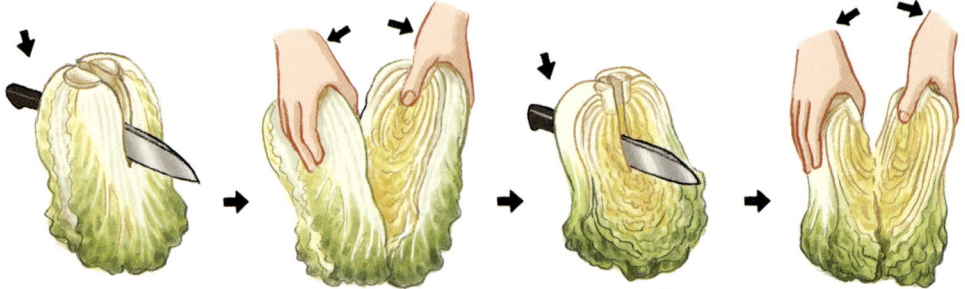

1 Remove the wilted leaves of the cabbage, cut the stem end in half, and pull apart to make two halves. Do the same for each half to make quarters. This will make less fragments.

2 Add 1 cup of salt to 2 liters of water to make salt water. Sprinkle on a 1/2 cup of salt to the tough white section of the cabbage and soak them in the salt water for 6 hours.

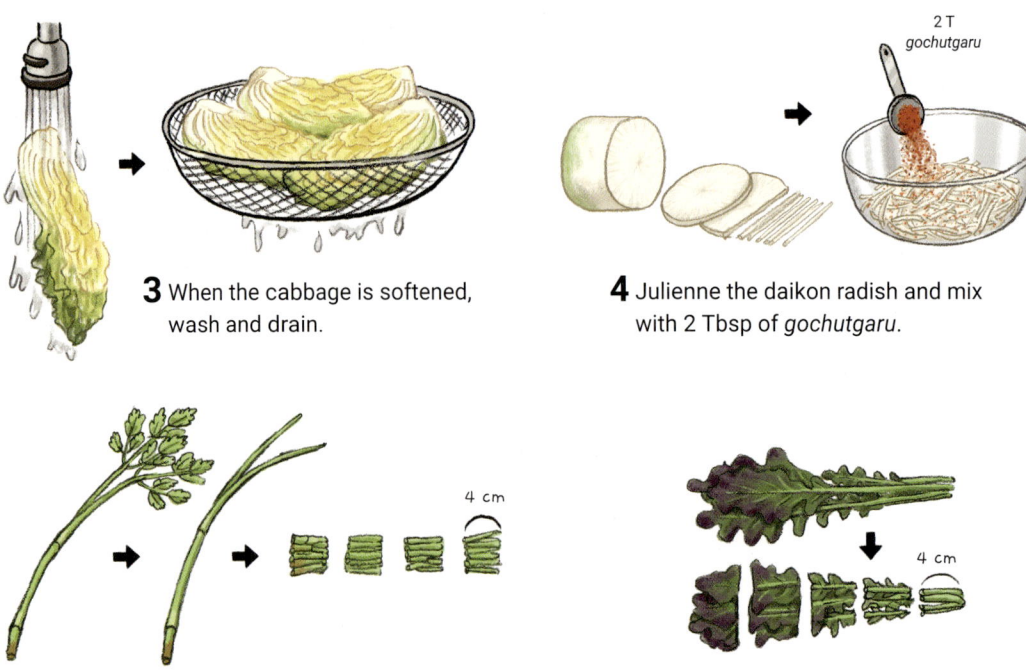

3 When the cabbage is softened, wash and drain.

4 Julienne the daikon radish and mix with 2 Tbsp of *gochutgaru*.

Remove the leaves of the water parsley and cut into 4 cm pieces.

Cut the mustard leaves into 4 cm pieces

Cut the small green onions into 4 cm pieces.

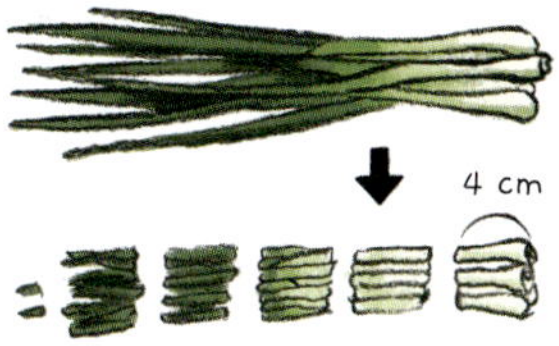

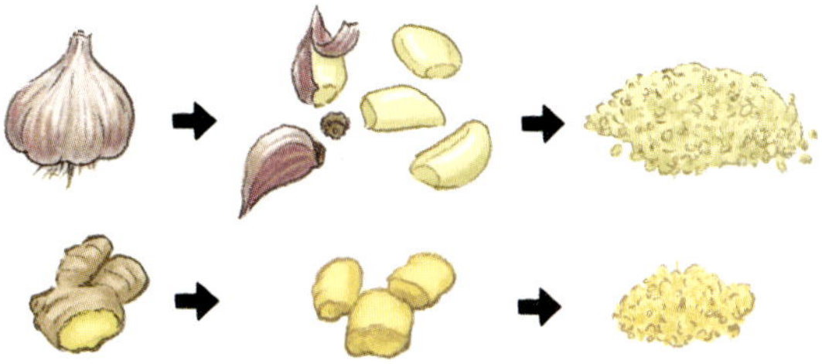

Mince garlic and ginger. (See p. 19.)

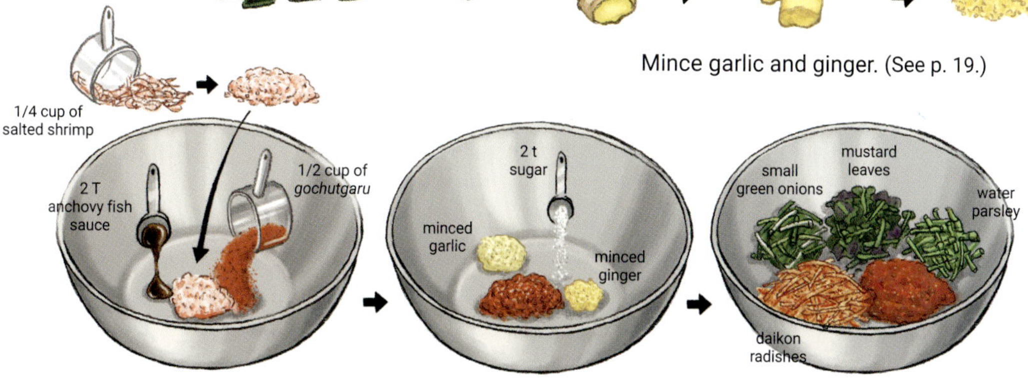

5 Mince the salted shrimp and mix with *gochutgaru* and anchovy fish sauce first. Add minced garlic, ginger, and sugar. Add some water if it's too thick.

6 Mix the sauce and step 4 in a bowl. Season with salt to make the paste.

7 Spread the paste over each leaf and wrap the cabbage quarter with the outer leaf. Transfer to a sealed container for storage. Rinse the bowl that contained the stuffing with 1 cup of water and 1 tsp of salt and pour over the kimchi. Close the lid and let it ferment. (The chili powder can make your hands itchy, so wear cooking gloves if you have them.)

Tips!

- The fermentation process will produce gas. It will overflow if the airtight container is too full. It is best to fill up to 80%.
- You can eat just-made kimchi but it needs about a month in the fridge to fully develop the flavors. Leaving fresh kimchi in room temperature for a day will make it ferment quickly.
- Make sure the kimchi doesn't come into contact with air. This will make develop other bacterias than lactic acid bacteria and it changes the flavor. Press down the cabbage so it is always submerged in the kimchi liquid.

Chapter 2
Side Dish
Banchan

깍두기
Kkakdugi

Diced Radish Kimchi

Daikon radishes are diced into small cubes, brined, drained and mixed with spicy kimchi seasoning. You can enjoy *kkakdugi* with any Korean meal, but it's especially good with a bowl of soup such as *seolleongtang* (beef bone soup) or *gukbap* (hot soup with rice). Fall season radish is sweet and firm which is just right for making *kkakdugi*.

Ingredients about 1.3 kg of *kkakdugi*

- 1 kg daikon radish
- 1 Tbsp salt
- 1 Tbsp sugar
- 50 g small green onion (*jjokpa*)
- 50 g water parsley

seasoning

- 3 Tbsp *gochutgaru*
- 1 Tbsp salted shrimp (*saeujeot*)
- 1 Tbsp minced garlic
- 1 tsp minced ginger
- 20 g onion

Mu (Daikon Radish)

Daikon radish is one of the most widely used vegetable in Korea. Aside from kimchi, you can also make *namul* (seasoned vegetables), *guk* (soup) and braised dishes with *mu*. The variety and also the different parts of the daikon radish each have their own flavor and uses. It has numerous health benefits such as preventing colds, improving digestion, curing hangovers, reducing cancer risk, and helping lose weight.

chonggak-kimchi (ponytail radish kimchi)

chonggakmu (ponytail radish)

mu (daikon radish)

mubineul-kimchi (daikon radish kimchi stuffed with spicy seasonings)

kkakdugi (daikon radish kimchi)

1 Wash the radish thoroughly. Cut into 2.5 cm x 2.5 cm x 3 cm cubes and brine with sugar and salt for 30 minutes. Transfer to a colander to drain.

Keep the drained water for later use.

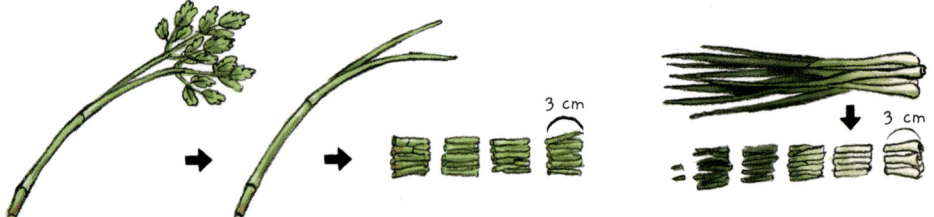

2 Remove the leaves from the water parsley, leaving only the stems and cut them into 3 cm sections. Cut the small green onions into 3 cm, also.

3 Mix radishes with *gochutgaru* first.

Mince salted shrimp and onion and add to the radishes with minced garlic and ginger.

Add water parsley, small green onions, and drained water from step 1, and then mix well. Transfer to a airtight container and store until fermented.

Tips!
- More water will come out as the kimchi ferments. Kimchi liquid can overflow if it's filled to the top, so make sure to fill the container only up to 80%.
- Leave it in room temperature to ferment for a day before storing it in the fridge. *Kkakdugi* ferments quicker than napa cabbage kimchi. It is better to eat soon.

Different types of kimchi

There are over 200 types of kimchi made of different vegetables including *baechu*-kimchi, *yeolmu*-kimchi, *pa*-kimchi, *kkakdugi*, *dongchimi*, *bossam*-kimchi, *buchu*-kimchi, *kkaennip*-kimchi, *oi-sobagi*, and *gat*-kimchi.

Baek-kimchi (White Kimchi)
This mild napa cabbage kimchi doesn't have *gochutgaru*. Instead, Asian pears, pine nuts, jujubes, and chestnuts are added. It's delicious kimchi to enjoy the crisp and fresh taste without the spicy flavor.

Pa-kimchi
(Green Onion Kimchi)

Jjokpa (small green onion) is mixed with salted anchovy sauce, salt, *gochutgaru*, garlic, and ginger. It can also be made with *silpa* (thread green onions), but *pa*-kimchi made with *jjokpa* harvested in early spring tastes better.

Bossam-kimchi (Wrapped Kimchi)
Napa cabbage, radish, small octopus, abalone, oyster, Asian pear, and pine nuts are mixed with spicy kimchi seasoning and wrapped with the cabbage leaves to make a small pouch. Made with various seafood and nut, this is considered to be the most refined and lavish of all kimchi varieties.

Dongchimi (Radish Water Kimchi)
Brined daikon radish is fermented with green onion, garlic, ginger, Asian pear, and seasoned water. You can eat it as a side dish or add noodles to enjoy it as *naengmyeon* (cold noodle). Daikon radish can be cut into a few pieces for spring and summer.

Kimchi Fermentation

Kimchi is fermented by a bacterium called lactobacillus. Most of the microorganisms are killed when the cabbage is brined, but lactic acid bacteria survive this process. As the kimchi ferments, the lactic acid bacteria produce lactic acid which gives kimchi's unique sour and refreshing taste.

Lactic acid bacteria boost digestive enzymes and suppress pathogen. It also helps excrete. Lactic acid bacteria proliferates when there's less air, so store kimchi in an airtight container or a sealed kimchi clay pot. In the old days, this traditional kimchi clay pot was buried in the ground to keep the kimchi stored at a cool temperature.

Now we have kimchi refrigerators for easy storage. It's the same principle as storing kimchi in clay pots buried in the ground for constant temperature maintenance.

Kimchi clay pots buried in the ground

Kimchi refrigerator

Chapter 2
Side Dish
Banchan

나박김치
Nabak-kimchi
Spicy Water Kimchi

Napa cabbage and daikon radish are cut into squares and fermented in seasoned liquid with green onions, garlic, ginger, and *gochutgaru*. It's very easy to make and can be eaten right after it's made. The refreshing and clean taste helps to regain your appetite in the summer.

Ingredients about 1.7 kg of *nabak*-kimchi

300 g napa cabbage	200 g daikon radish	30 g water parsley	10 cm green onion (white part)	1 red chili
		3 cloves garlic	7 g ginger	1 Tbsp salt

kimchi liquid

6 cups of water · 1 Tbsp *gochutgaru* · 2 Tbsp salt · 1 Tbsp flour

What is *mul*-kimchi (water kimchi)?

It is a mild and refreshing type of kimchi made with daikon radishes and napa cabbage and seasoned water. *Dongchimi* (radish water kimchi), *nabak*-kimchi (water kimchi), *jang*-kimchi (vegetable kimchi in soy sauce), *yeolmu mul*-kimchi (young summer radish water kimchi), and *dolnamul*-kimchi (sedum spicy water kimchi) are all different types of *mul*-kimchi.

dongchimi *jang*-kimchi *yeolmu mul*-kimchi *dolnamul*-kimchi

---

Food that goes well with *mul*-kimchi

You can eat *mul*-kimchi with a bowl of rice, but it also goes well with carbohydrate food such as *tteok* (rice cake), *tteokguk* (rice cake soup), noodles and sweet potatoes. The lactic acid bacteria in kimchi promotes digestion and keeps the intestinal walls clean.

Sweet potatoes and ***mul-kimchi*** are a perfect pair!

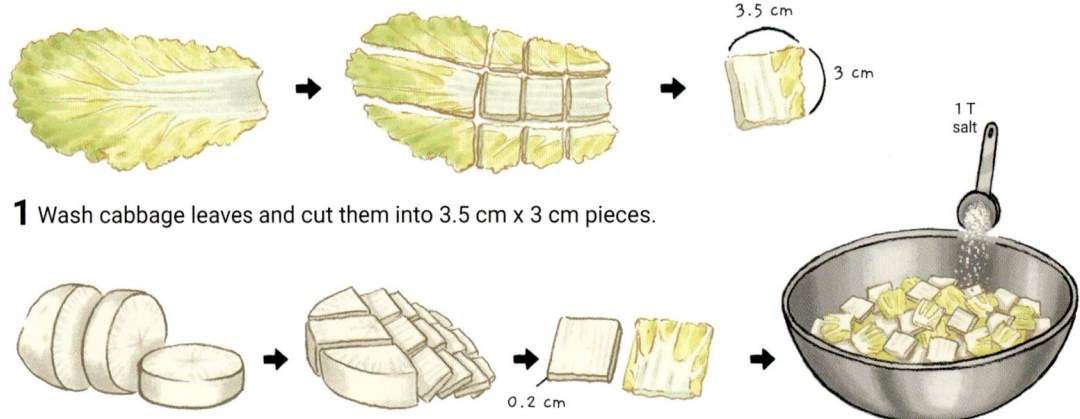

1 Wash cabbage leaves and cut them into 3.5 cm x 3 cm pieces.

2 Choose a firm daikon radish, wash and cut into smaller pieces than cabbage, about 0.2 cm thick. Mix radishes and cabbage with 1 Tsp salt and leave for 20 minutes.

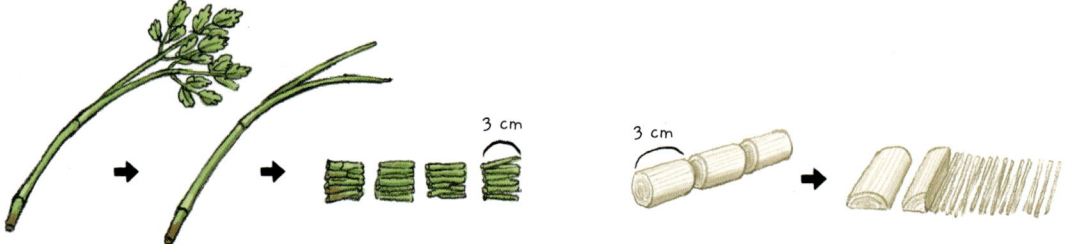

3 Cut the water parsley stems into 3 cm.

4 Cut the white part of green onion into 3 cm sections and thinly slice.

5 Julienne garlic and ginger.

6 Boil 5 cups of water in a pot. Mix 1 cup of water and 1 Tbsp flour in a bowl. Add the flour mixture to the boiling water with salt and turn off the heat.

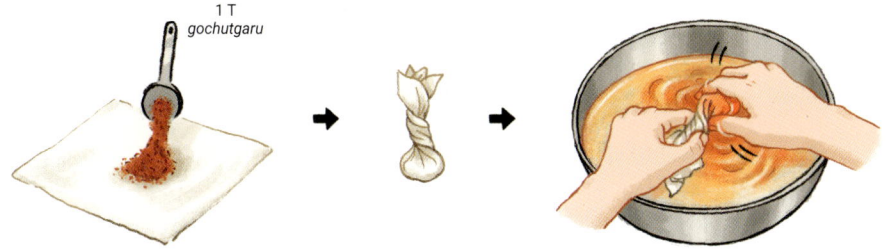

When the liquid is cooled, wrap *gochutgaru* with a cotton cooking cloth and dissolve in the liquid. If the *gochutgaru* is fine, simply mix in the water.

7 Julienne the red chili into 3 cm.

8 Mix the sliced red chilis with radishes and cabbage and add green onions, garlic, ginger, and water parsley. Pour kimchi liquid from step 6 into the vegetables. (Adjust the amount of the liquid.)

Tips!
- Leave the water kimchi in room temperature to ferment for a day. Store in the fridge.
- The flour liquid gives water kimchi a delicious sweet flavor when fermented. If you're not using flour mixture, add 1 Tbsp of sugar instead.

Kimchi and chilis in Korean food

Kimchi was originally white but slowly became red and spicy after chilis were introduced to Korea in the mid 1600s. Kimchi made with red chilis and fish sauce is recorded in *Kyuhapchongseo*, an early 19th century guide to homemaking book. Since then, more chili was added to kimchi and a wider variety of spicy dishes were created as people became accustomed to the spicy flavor.

Capsaicin, the compound that gives chili its spiciness, reduces the fishy smell of fish sauce and prevents fat from going rancid. It also helps lactic acid bacteria to ferment well and prevents the loss of vitamin C of vegetables and chilis in kimchi. The red color of chilis also stimulates the appetite. All in all, kimchi is a traditional health food created by old wisdom and experience.

Chapter 2
Side Dish
Banchan

삼색나물
Samsaek-namul
Three Seasoned Vegetables

Side dishes made with foraged or harvested vegetables are all called *namul*. This *samsaek-namul* dish is made with three different colored vegetables served together on one plate.

Ingredients 2 servings

spinach namul (sigeumchinamul)

- 200 g spinach
- 1/2 tsp salt

seasoning
- 1/2 tsp soy sauce (*jip-ganjang*)
- 1 tsp sesame seeds
- 1 tsp sesame oil
- 1 tsp minced green onion
- 1/2 tsp mince garlic

julienne radish fresh salad (*musaengchae*)

- 200 g daikon radish

seasoning
- 2 tsp gochutgaru
- 1/2 tsp salt
- 1 tsp sugar
- 2 tsp vinegar
- 1/2 tsp minced green onion
- 1/2 tsp minced garlic

bean (or mung bean) sprouts namul (*kongnamul* or *sukjunamul*)

- 200 g bean sprouts (or mung bean sprouts)
- 1/4 tsp salt

seasoning
- 1 tsp soy sauce (*jip-ganjang*)
- 1 tsp sesame seeds
- 1 tsp sesame oil
- 1/2 tsp minced green onion
- 1/2 tsp minced garlic

Korean *Namul*

Korea has four distinct seasons, producing diverse vegetables and herbs. Therefore, a wide variety of *namul* has been well developed using most of vegetables and mushrooms, sprouts of trees, and fruit vegetables such as cucumber, eggplant, and zucchini.

Methods for making *namul*

Stir-fried — sweet potato stem *namul*

Blanched — pimpinella *namul*

Fresh — Korean chive fresh *namul*

Dried and Rehydrated — taro stem *namul*, fernbrake *namul*

1 Remove wilted leaves of the spinach, divide into small sections and wash.

2 Boil water enough to sink all spinach and add salt. Blanch the spinach for 1 minute. Rinse in cold water and squeeze out the water. Cut into 2 to 3 sections if the leaves are big.

3 Mix the seasoning ingredients and season the spinach.

4 Wash and peel the daikon radish and julienne into thin pieces. Mix with *gochutgaru*.

5 Mix the seasoning ingredients and add to the radishes just before serving.

6 Pour 1 cup of water and 1/4 tsp salt into a pan and add the washed bean sprouts. Close the lid and cook for 5 minutes.

7 Drain the cooked bean sprouts and mix with the seasonings. (If using mung bean sprouts, blanch them briefly and season.)

8 Arrange the three seasoned vegetables on a plate and garnish with sesame seeds.

Special Dish

These dishes are made on special occasions such as parties, birthdays, and other celebrations. The recipes can be tricky, but the dishes are delicious and beautifully made and nutritious. It can be enjoyed as a single dish, but it is customary to serve it with main dishes and side dishes in Korean cuisine.

Sinseollo (Royal Hot Pot)

Gujeolpan (Platter of Nine Delicacies)

Japchae (Stir-fried Glass Noodles and Vegetables)

Gungjung-tteokbokki (Royal Stir-fried Rice Cakes)

Samgyetang (Ginseng Chicken Soup)

Bossam (Napa Wraps with Pork)

Chapter 3
Special Dish

Chapter 3
Special Dish

신선로
Sinseollo

Royal Hot Pot

Sinseollo is the name of this elaborate dish as well as the pot it is served in. It is also known as *yeolgujatang* which means "the soup that makes your mouth happy." Small pieces of charcoal are placed in the pole in the center of the pot and various ingredients such as meat, fish, and vegetables are colorfully arranged around the pot. It is decorated with nuts and a rich broth is poured over the ingredients and cooked on the table. *Sinseollo* is the most representative and impressive dish among the elegant and luxurious royal court cuisine.

Ingredients for 20 cm in diameter *sinseollo* casserole/4 servings

- 150 g beef (shin shank, brisket)
- 100 g daikon radish
- 100 g carrot
- 1 piece of kelp (10 cm x 10 cm)
- 50 g omasum
- 100 g white fish fillets
- 100 g beef rump
- 30 g tofu
- 1 red chili
- 3 dried shiitake mushrooms
- 3 manna lichen mushrooms
- 50 g water parsley
- 12 ginkgo nuts
- 5 half walnuts
- 1 tsp pine nuts
- 5 eggs
- 1/2 cup of flour
- a drizzle of cooking oil

beef marinade

- 1 Tbsp soy sauce (*yangjo-ganjang*)
- 1 tsp sugar
- 1 tsp minced green onion
- 1/2 tsp minced garlic
- 1/2 tsp sesame seeds
- 1/2 tsp sesame oil
- a pinch of black pepper

broth (5 cups)

- 6 cups of water
- 1 Tbsp soy sauce (*jip-ganjang*)
- a pinch of salt
- a pinch of sugar
- a pinch of black pepper

Jeongol (Hot Pot)

Beef broth is poured over the ingredients laid out in a shallow pot and cooked at the table. Diners share this dish together and enjoy the cooked ingredients that are kept warm throughout the meal.

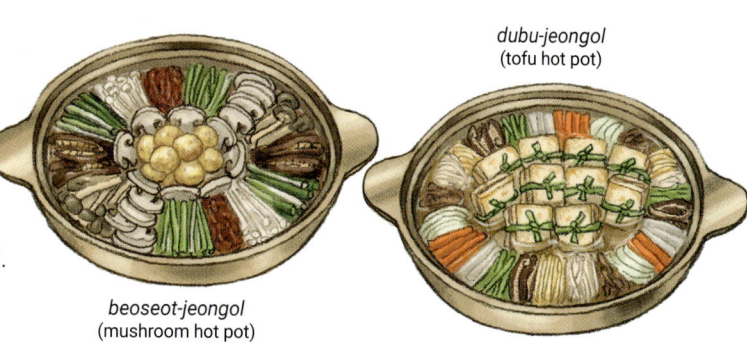

beoseot-jeongol (mushroom hot pot)

dubu-jeongol (tofu hot pot)

1 Boil beef brisket, daikon radish, carrot, and kelp with 6 cups of water. Remove the kelp when the water boils.

Remove the carrot and daikon radish 5 minutes later.

After 20 minutes, remove the beef and pour the broth over a cotton cooking cloth and season.

2 Thinly slice the boiled beef brisket and cut the radish and carrot into 0.3 cm thick, 2 cm wide pieces to fit into the pot.

3 Make the marinade for the beef.

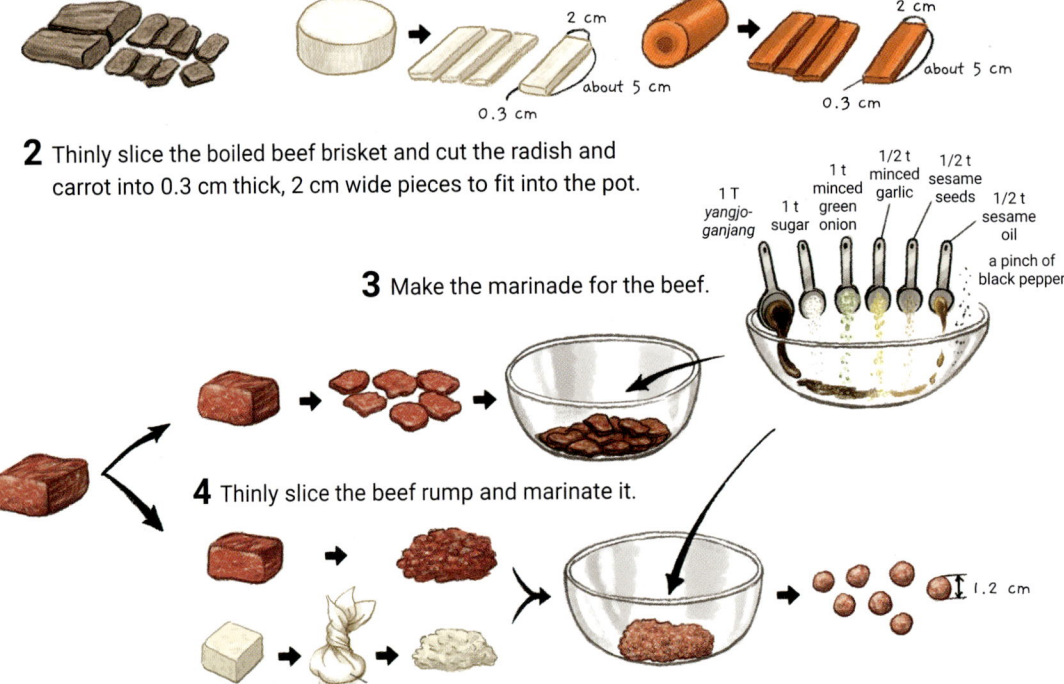

4 Thinly slice the beef rump and marinate it.

5 Mince the other half of the rump and marinate it. Mix with tofu (water squeezed out and minced) and shape into small balls 1.2 cm in diameter.

Coat with flour and beaten eggs. Sauté in a pan.

manna lichen mushrooms   hot water

6 Take 3 eggs and separate the egg white and yolk, and pan-fry the yolk to make *jidan*. Use half of the egg white to make *jidan*. To make black *jidan*, soak the manna lichen mushrooms in hot water, wash, and mince. Add this to the remaining half of the egg white. Cut into 2 cm wide pieces. (See p. 21 for *jidan*.)

7 Making *minarichodae* (pan-fried water parsley) Skewer the stems of the water parsley without the leaves. Coat with flour and eggs and pan-fry. Cut into 2 cm wide, 5 cm long pieces.

salt   black pepper

8 Season white fish fillets with salt and pepper. Coat with flour and eggs then pan-fry. Cut into 2 cm wide, 5 cm long pieces.

9 Wash the omasum with salt and flour and blanch. Scrape the outer black part with a knife and make shallow cuts. Season with salt and pepper and coat with flour and eggs and pan-fry. Cut into 2 cm wide, 5 cm long pieces.

10 Soak the shiitake mushrooms remove the stem. Slice into 2 cm wide pieces. Remove the seeds of the red chili and cut into the same size.

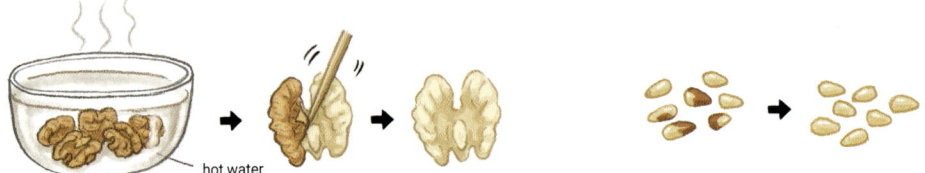

11 Soak the walnuts in hot water and peel the skin. Clean the pine nuts.

12 Peel the outer skin of the ginkgo nuts and pan-fry with oil. Rub with a paper towel to peel off the inner skin.

13 Lay some of the daikon radishes and carrots on the bottom of the pot.

Top with the sliced beef brisket from step 2.

Lay marinated beef from step 4 on top of it.

Arrange the 2 cm wide cooked ingredients around the pot matching colors.

Garnish with walnuts, pine nuts, ginkgo nuts, and meatballs.

Pour in the broth.

Close the lid and put hot charcoals into the pole.
(In case of using solid fuel, use it in a container.)
Serve with small bowls and a ladle.

Chapter 3
Special
Dish

구절판
Gujeolpan
Platter of Nine Delicacies

Gujeolpan is a beautiful dish with nine compartments filled with crepe-like wheat flour pancakes and eight other meat and vegetable ingredients. The fillings are wrapped in the flour pancakes for individual servings. The ingredients for the fillings are selected to represent the five Korean traditional colors, *obangsaek*. *Gujeolpan* makes a great table centerpiece for parties and pairs well with any type of liquor.

Ingredients 2 servings

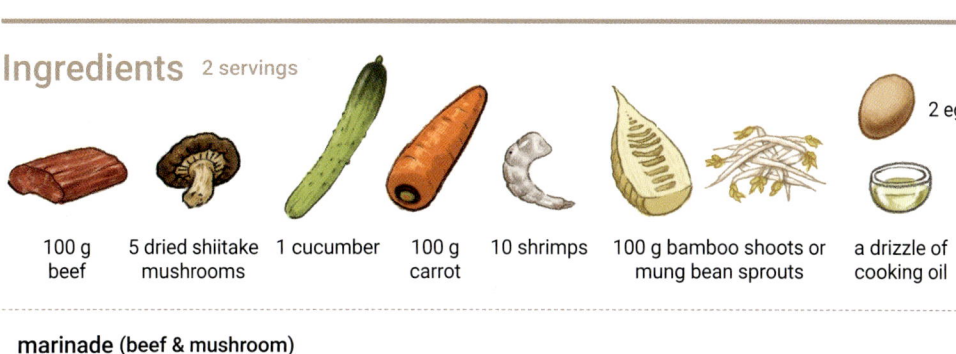

| 100 g beef | 5 dried shiitake mushrooms | 1 cucumber | 100 g carrot | 10 shrimps | 100 g bamboo shoots or mung bean sprouts | a drizzle of cooking oil | a pinch of salt | 2 eggs |

marinade (beef & mushroom)

- 2 Tbsp soy sauce (*yangjo-ganjang*)
- 1/2 Tbsp sugar
- 1 Tbsp minced green onion
- 1 tsp minced garlic
- 2 tsp sesame oil
- 1/4 tsp sesame seeds
- a pinch of black pepper

flour pancakes

- 1 cup of flour
- 1/2 tsp salt
- 1 1/4 cups of water
- 1 Tbsp pine nuts

mustard sauce

- 2 Tbsp mustard seed powder
- 1 Tbsp warm water
- 1 Tbsp vinegar
- 1 Tbsp sugar
- 1/4 tsp salt

dipping sauce (soy-vinegar)

- 4 Tbsp soy sauce (*yangjo-ganjang*)
- 2 Tbsp vinegar
- 1 Tbsp water
- small pinch of sugar

Gujeolpan is the name of the dish as well as the platter it is served in. The wooden platter is usually lacquered and beautifully decorated with inlaid mother-of-pearl. You can also find earthenware platters or ones made with plastic, glass, or brass.

1 Make the marinade sauce.

2 T yangjo-ganjang · 1/2 T sugar · 1 T minced green onion · 1 t minced garlic · 2 t sesame oil · 1/4 t sesame seeds · a pinch of black pepper

2 Finely slice the soaked shiitake mushroom with the stem removed and marinate it. Finely slice the beef and marinate it.

3 Sauté the mushroom and beef separately.

4 Cut the cucumber into 5 cm sections and cut each section into thin sheets, removing the seed part and julienne. Sprinkle with salt, squeeze out the water and sauté. Spread and let it cool quickly.

5 Julienne the carrot into 5 cm length and sauté with a small pinch of salt.

6 Julienne the bamboo shoots into 5 cm length and sauté with a small pinch of salt.

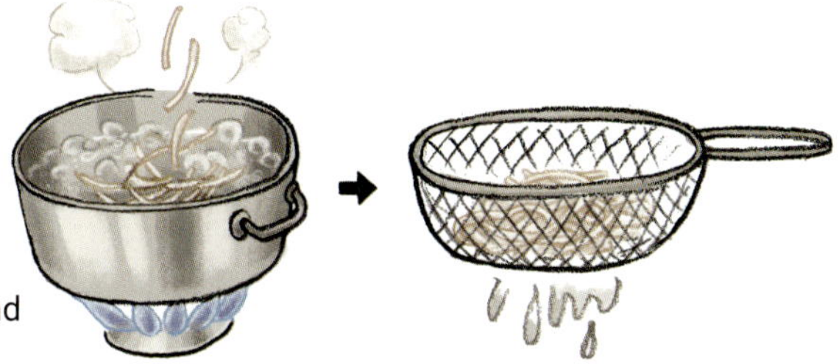

If using mung bean sprouts, remove the head and tail end, blanch and drain the water.

7 Separate the egg white and yolk and pan-fry. (See p. 21 for *jidan*.) Julienne into 5 cm length.

8 Boil the shrimp and peel the shell. Cut it lengthwise.

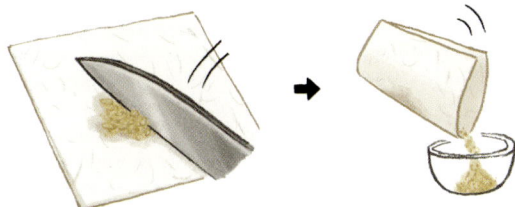

9 Mince the pine nuts on top of a sheet of paper to absorb the oil. (See p. 22 for pine nut powder.)

161

10 Mix flour, salt, and water and pour through a sieve. In a pan with oil, put a spoon of batter to make a thin pancake roughly 8 cm in diameter. (Make it very thin for better texture.) Sprinkle with pine nut powder and stack them together.

11 Mix mustard powder with warm water, seal with a lid and keep it warm for 10 minutes to enhance the spicy flavor. Add vinegar, sugar, and salt to make the mustard sauce.

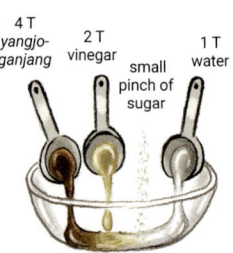

12 Make the soy-vinegar dipping sauce.

13 Place the pancakes in the middle compartment of the platter and arrange the rest of the ingredients around the pancakes.

Serve with mustard sauce and soy-vinegar dipping sauce.

Chapter 3
Special Dish

잡채

Japchae

Stir-fried Glass Noodles and Vegetables

Japchae is a vegetable-based dish made with boiled and stir-fried glass noodles mixed with various vegetables, mushrooms, and meat. It was originally made with more vegetables and less glass noodles, but glass noodles are added more these days. This nutritious and colorful dish is a popular party food made on special occasions and holidays.

Ingredients 4 servings

100 g glass noodles	100 g beef	3 dried shiitake mushrooms	10 g dried wood ear mushroom	100 g onion
50 g carrot	70 g cucumber	50 g mung bean sprouts	1 egg	a pinch of salt / a drizzle of cooking oil

marinade (beef & mushroom)

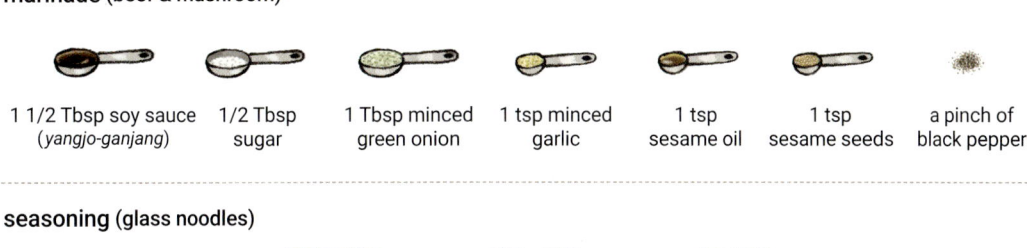

1 1/2 Tbsp soy sauce (*yangjo-ganjang*) · 1/2 Tbsp sugar · 1 Tbsp minced green onion · 1 tsp minced garlic · 1 tsp sesame oil · 1 tsp sesame seeds · a pinch of black pepper

seasoning (glass noodles)

1 Tbsp soy sauce (*yangjo-ganjang*) · 1 Tbsp sugar · 1 tsp sesame oil

---

Japchae is made in large portions on celebrations. Boiled glass noodles will become sticky and lose its elastic texture over time. A way to prevent this is to soak the noodles in water and stir-fry it.

What is *dangmyeon* (glass noodles)?

Korean glass noodles called *dangmyeon* are made with sweet potato, potato, or corn starch. It goes through kneading, noodle making, gelatinization, refrigeration, defrosting, and drying. It was made with mung bean starch in the past, but the glass noodles manufactured these days are made with a mix of various starch.

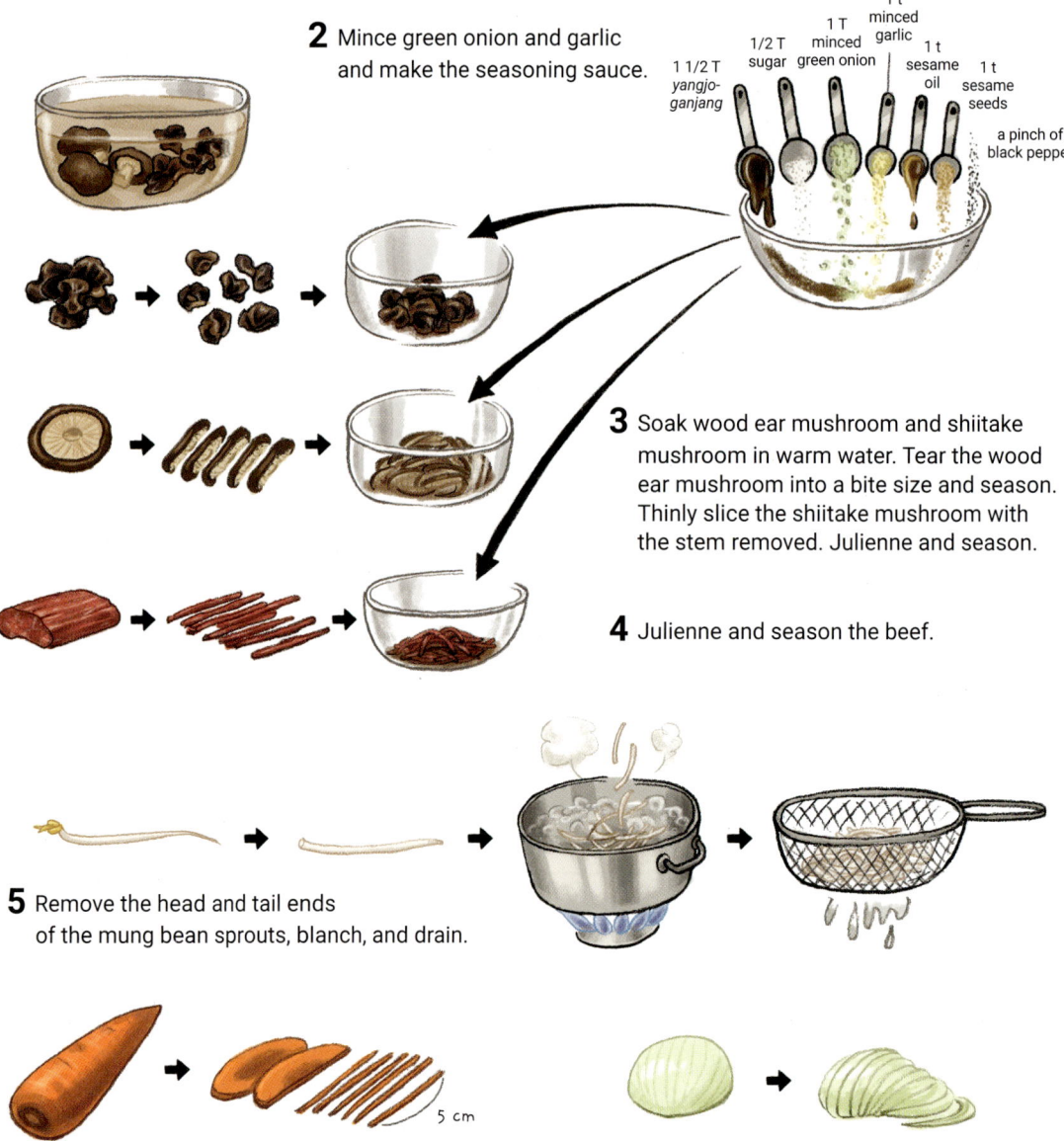

1 Cut the cucumber into 6 cm sections and cut each section into thin sheets, removing the seed part. Julienne into 0.3 cm x 0.3 cm x 6 cm pieces, sprinkle with salt and squeeze out the water using cotton cooking cloth.

2 Mince green onion and garlic and make the seasoning sauce.

3 Soak wood ear mushroom and shiitake mushroom in warm water. Tear the wood ear mushroom into a bite size and season. Thinly slice the shiitake mushroom with the stem removed. Julienne and season.

4 Julienne and season the beef.

5 Remove the head and tail ends of the mung bean sprouts, blanch, and drain.

6 Julienne the carrot into 5 cm pieces and julienne the onion.

7 Separate egg white and yolk and pan-fry to make *jidan*. Julienne into 5 cm length. (See p. 21 for *jidan*.)

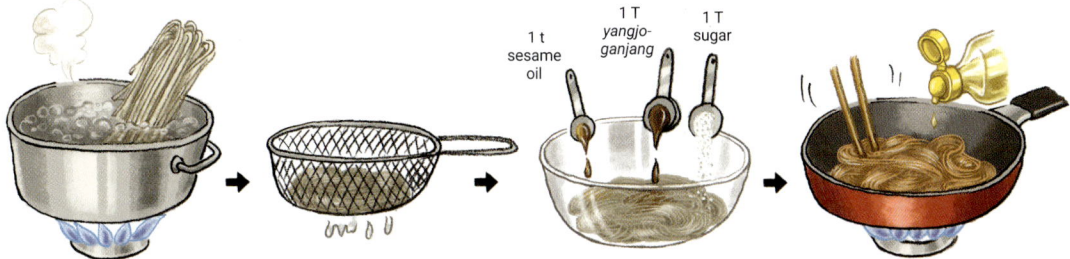

8 Boil 4 cups of water to a pot and add glass noodles.
When the water boils again, cook for 5 minutes in low heat until the noodles become transparent.
Drain the noodles in a colander, season with the noodle seasoning and stir-fry in a frying pan with oil.

9 In a pan, individually stir-fry the ingredients in the following order: cucumber, onion, carrot, ear mushroom, shiitake mushroom, and beef.

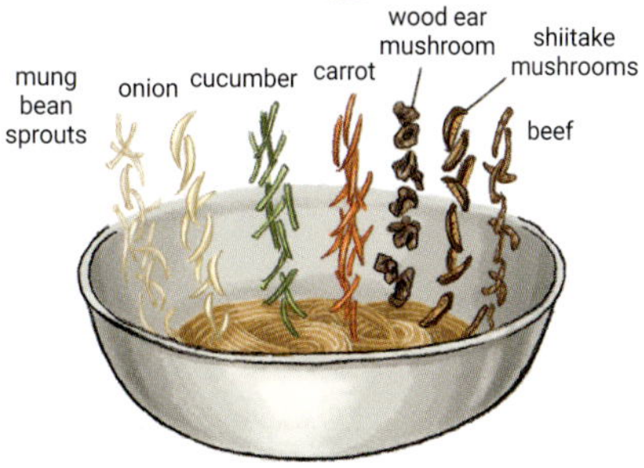

10 Mix the noodles and cooked ingredients in a large bowl.

Finish with black pepper and a drizzle of sesame oil.
Garnish with the white and yellow *jidan* and serve.

Chapter 3
Special
Dish

궁중떡볶이
Gungjung-tteokbokki
Royal Stir-fried Rice Cakes

Long cylinders of white rice cake are stir-fried in a soy sauce-based sauce with various vegetables for this savory dish that enjoyed at the Joseon court. This nutritionally well-balanced dish can be enjoyed as a simple meal.

Ingredients 2 servings

300 g *garaettok* (long rice cake)	50 g beef	10 g dried shiitake mushroom	150 g onion	30 g water parsley
50 g carrot	50 g mung bean sprouts	1 egg	a drizzle of cooking oil	1/3 tsp salt
2 tsp sesame oil				

marinade (beef & mushroom)

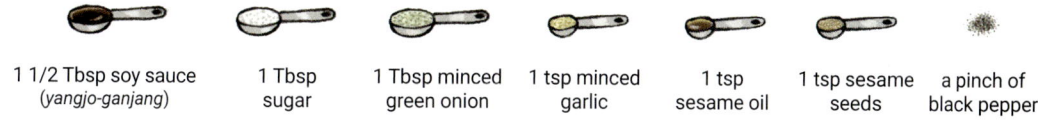

- 1 1/2 Tbsp soy sauce (*yangjo-ganjang*)
- 1 Tbsp sugar
- 1 Tbsp minced green onion
- 1 tsp minced garlic
- 1 tsp sesame oil
- 1 tsp sesame seeds
- a pinch of black pepper

Different types of *garaetteok*
(cylinder-shaped white rice cake)

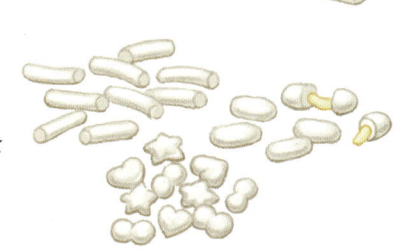

For *tteokguk* (rice cake soup): Thick *garaetteok* is sliced into small 3 cm wide discs to make rice cake soup. This type of *garaetteok* can be sliced lengthwise into quarters for making *tteokbokki*.

For *tteokbokki* (stir-fried rice cake): About 1/4 of thick *garaetteok* is cut into 5 cm to 6 cm pieces to make *tteokbokki*. You can also find *tteok* in different shapes or ones filled with cheese or sweet potato.

You can make *tteok-jjim* (braised rice cake), *tteok-sanjeok* (race cake skewered), or *tteokbokki* (stir-fried rice cake) with *garaetteok*.

On Lunar New Year's Day, small circles of *tteok* are cooked with beef broth to make *tteokguk* (rice cake soup). Families came together to share a bowl of *tteokguk*, and wished for good health and prosperity in the new year. These days manufactured and sliced one from stores are used.

Tteokguk
(Rice Cake Soup)

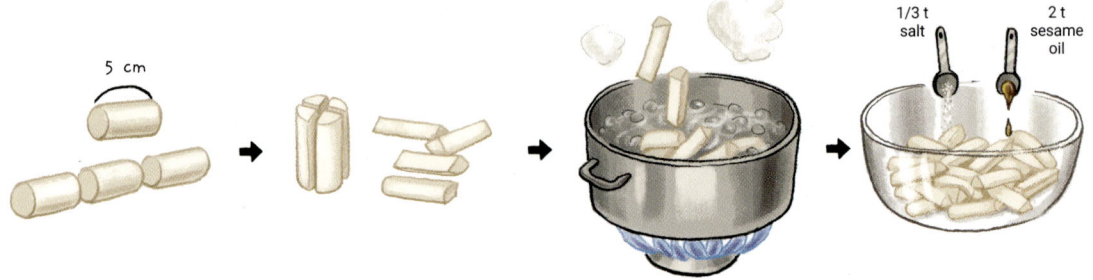

1 Cut the *garaetteok* into 5 cm length and quarter them.
   Boil the *tteok* to soften them and season with salt and sesame oil.

2 Mince green onion and garlic and make the seasoning sauce.

3 Soak the shiitake mushroom, julienne and season it.

4 Julienne the beef and season it.

5 Cut the stems of water parsley into 5 cm length.

6 Remove the head and tail ends of the mung bean sprout, blanch, and drain.

7 Julienne onion and carrot.

8 Sauté onion and carrot separately with cooking oil in a pan.

9 Separate egg white and yolk and pan-fry to make *jidan*. Julienne into 5 cm length. (See p. 21 for *jidan*.)

10 Stir-fry the beef and shiitake mushroom together in an oiled pan and add carrot, onion, and *tteok*.

Add water parsley and mung bean sprout. Stir-fry lightly.

11 Garnish with the white and yellow *jidan* and serve.

Chapter 3
Special
Dish

삼계탕
Samgyetang
Ginseng Chicken Soup

A whole chicken is stuffed with ginseng, glutinous rice, dried jujube, garlic, and chestnut and slow cooked in a pot. This is an iconic nourishing food that helps fight the summer heat. Many Koreans eat *samgyetang* at least once before the summer passes by.

Ingredients 1 serving

- 1 whole chicken (500 g)
- 1/3 cup of glutinous rice
- 1 root ginseng
- 2 chestnuts
- 1 stem of thread green onion (*silpa*)
- 2 dried jujubes
- 2 cloves garlic
- 5 cups of water
- small pinch of salt
- small pinch of black pepper

In the olden days when a son-in-law comes for a visit, the mother-in-law would cook a meal with the chicken she had been raising. Mothers treated their sons-in-law as special guests with hopes that their daughters would live happily with their husbands. According to *Donguibogam*, the yellow Korean hen protects the five major organs, fills the bone marrow, revitalizes the body and keeps the small intestine warm. The ginseng gives energy, strengthens the spleen and lungs, quenches the thirst, and helps to calm the mind. That is probably why this precious health food was cooked and served to sons-in-law.

Make **dakjuk** (chicken porridge) with leftover *samgyetang*!

Shred remaining chicken into the *samgyetang* soup, add soaked glutinous rice or white rice, and boil. Season with salt and you get a delicious chicken porridge.

Dakjuk
(Chicken Porridge)

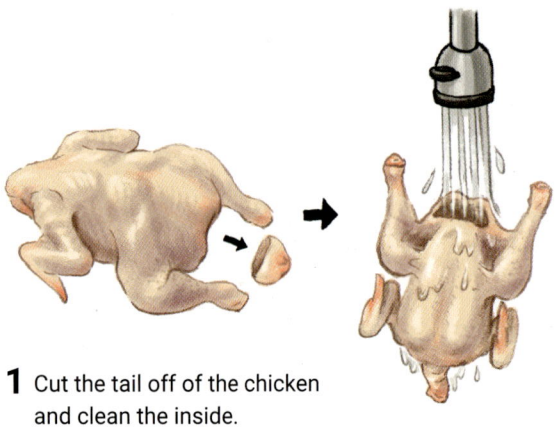

1 Cut the tail off of the chicken and clean the inside.

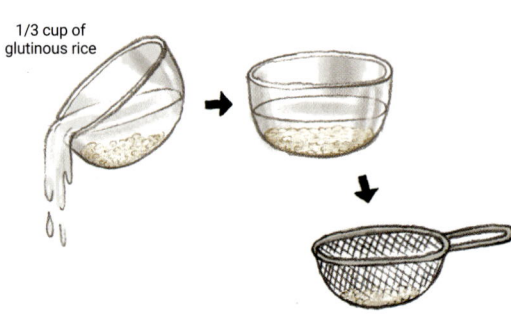

2 Wash glutinous rice and soak for at least 30 minutes. Pour through a colander and drain.

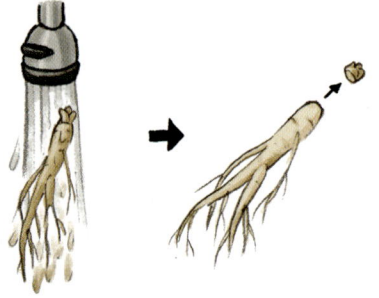

3 Thoroughly clean unpeeled ginseng and cut off the top.

Clean dried jujubes including the inner seams.

4 Peel chestnuts including inner skin.

Cut off ends of garlics and wash.

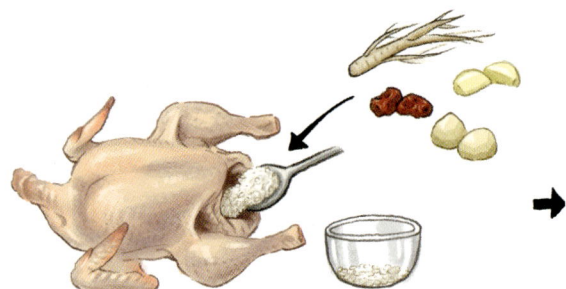

5 Stuff glutinous rice, ginseng, jujubes, chestnuts, and garlics into the chicken.

Tie the legs with cooking string to keep the stuffing inside and flip the ends of the wings towards the back. (Place the chicken as it is in a pot.)

6 Add water in the pot.

Keep the lid partially opened to prevent the soup from boiling over and cook in medium heat for 20 minutes.

Remove foam while cooking.

Reduce to low heat and cook for 20 minutes with lid slightly opened.

7 Chop green onions and serve it in a small bowl along with salt and pepper.

Chapter 3
Special
Dish

보쌈
Bossam
Napa Wraps with Pork

For this dish, boiled pork is dipped in salted shrimp and wrapped in napa cabbage leaves with some spicy daikon radish and Asian pear salad. Boiled pork with salted shrimp was enjoyed since the old days, but wrapping it in salted cabbage was a new method introduced by restaurants in the late 1900s. *Bossam* is served as à la carte in restaurants, but it can also be a great *banchan* (side dish) or *anju* (food consumed with alcohol).

Ingredients 4 servings

- 1 kg pork belly
- 1 Tbsp *doenjang* (soybean paste)
- 10 cm green onion
- 3 cloves garlic
- 1 clove ginger
- 5 cups of water

pickled napa cabbage
- 300 g napa cabbage
- 3 Tbsp salt
- 3 cups of water

julienne radish fresh salad (*musaengchae*)
- 300 g daikon radish
- 1 Tbsp salt
- 1/4 Asian pear

seasoning
- 2 Tbsp *gochutgaru*
- 1 1/2 Tbsp sugar
- 1 tsp salt
- 1 Tbsp minced garlic
- 2 Tbsp minced green onion
- 2 tsp minced ginger

shrimp sauce seasoning
- 3 Tbsp salted shrimp (*saeujeot*)
- 1 Tbsp vinegar
- 1/2 tsp *gochutgaru*

Whole chunk of boiled pork is called *suyuk*, and it is sliced to make *pyeonyuk*.

Ssam

Ssam means "to wrap," and it has a symbolic meaning to "wrap good fortune." Any leafy vegetable with large leaves can be used for making *ssam*, but Koreans' favorite is lettuce wraps.

Spread a lettuce leaf on your palm and add rice or meat and season with *gochujang*, *doenjang,* or *ssamjang*. (See p. 16.) Perilla leaves, napa cabbage, groundsei, and fresh kelp can be eaten as they are, and pumpkin leaves are steamed before using as wraps.

177

1 For the napa cabbage, use the yellow leaves from the middle, and soak in salt water for 30 minutes, turning over occasionally. When softened, rinse and drain.

2 Add green onion, garlic, ginger, *doenjang* to a pot with enough water to cover the meat. Add meat when the water boils.

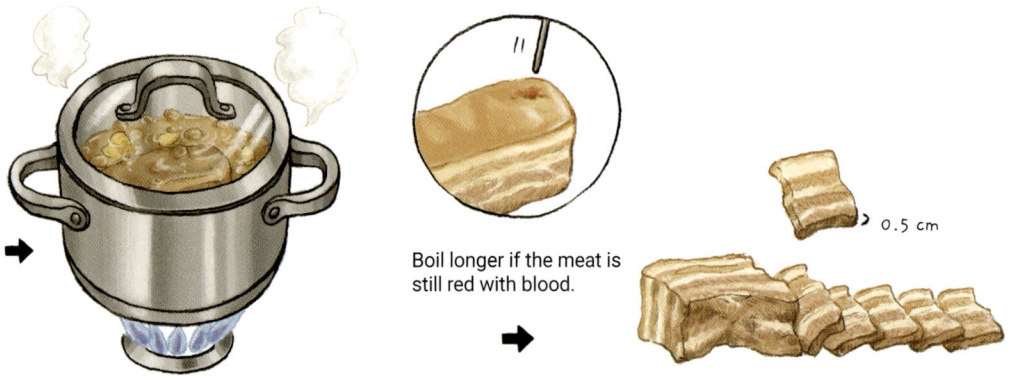

Boil longer if the meat is still red with blood.

Boil for more than 30 minutes in medium heat. Check to see if the meat is cooked through by poking it with a chopstick. If the meat is cooked, take it out and cut into 0.5 cm thick pieces.

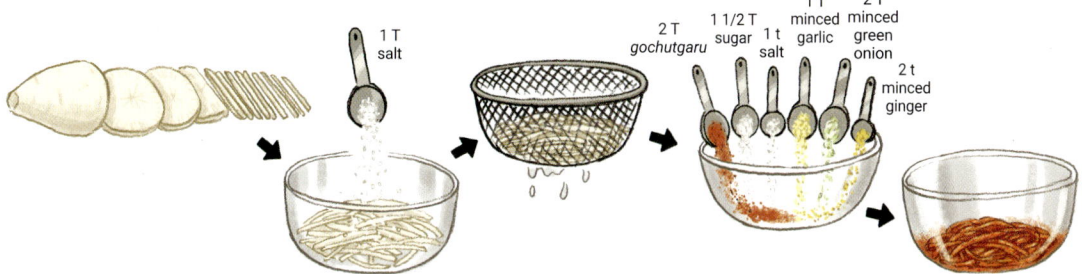

3 Julienne the daikon radish, brine, and drain in a colander. Mix with seasoning sauce.

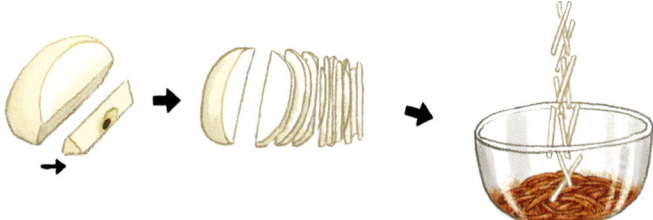

Peel the Asian pear and julienne. Add it to the seasoned radish to make the salad.

4 Use only the shrimp from the salted shrimp and mince. Add *gochutgaru* and vinegar to make sauce.

5 Serve cabbage leaves, radish salad, and sliced pork on a plate with the shrimp sauce.

Samgyeopsal-gui (Grilled Pork Belly)

Grilling is also a popular way to enjoy this cut in Korea. Take a piece of grilled pork and wrap in a lettuce or perilla leaf with *ssamjang*. You can also add some rice or grilled kimchi, onion, mushroom, and garlic to the wrap.

Dessert & Drink

Korean traditional dessert and drinks are made with seasonal ingredients and usually served with fresh fruit. It is traditionally placed on the table with the main dishes, but nowadays, it is served after the meal.

Baekseolgi (Snow White Rice Cake)

Hwajeon (Pan-fried Flower Rice Cake)

Omija-hwachae (Omija Punch)

Sujeonggwa (Cinnamon Punch)

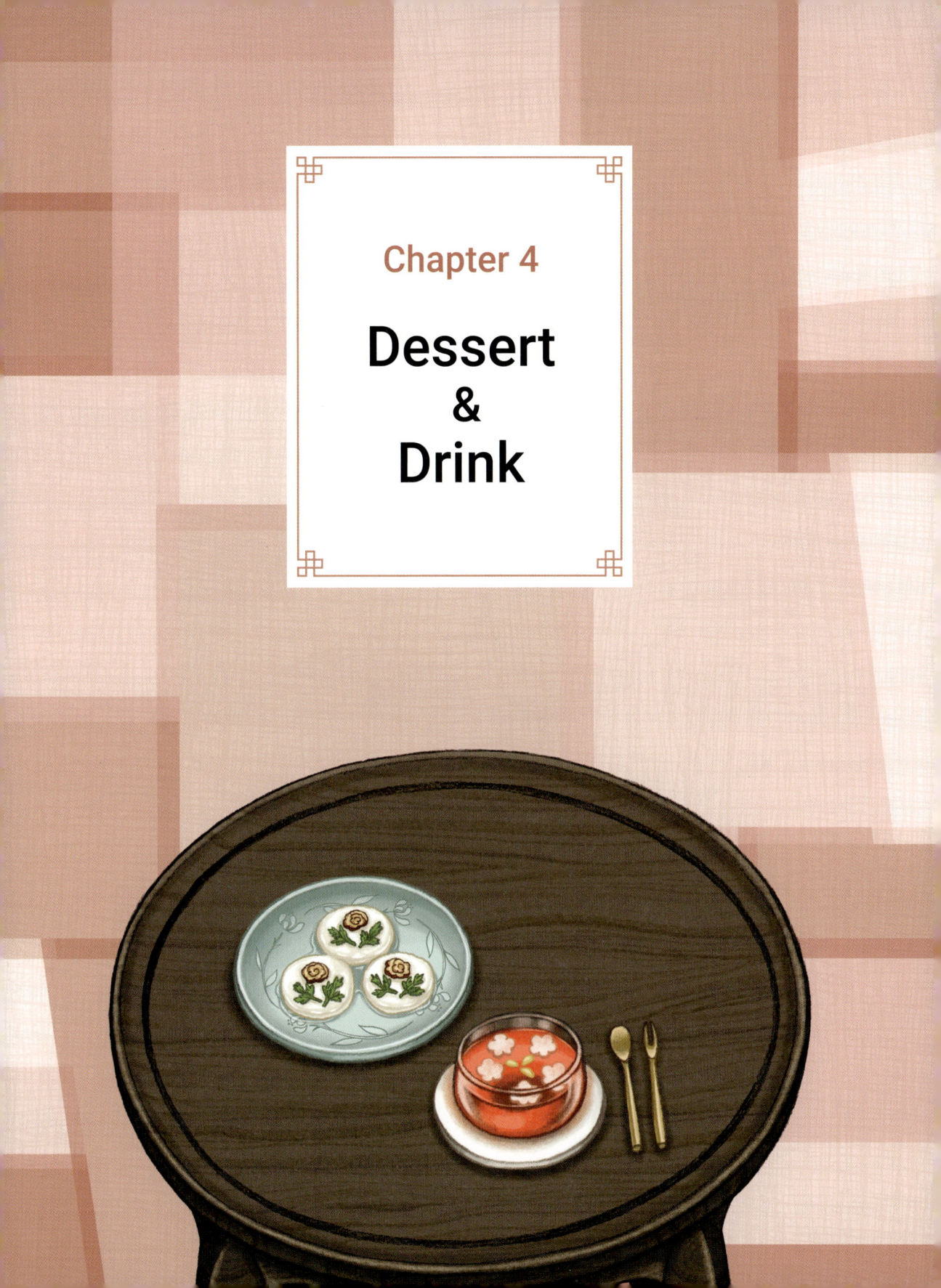

> Chapter 4
> Dessert & Drink

백설기
Baekseolgi

Snow White Rice Cake

White rice powder is mixed with sugar water and steamed in *siru* (traditional steamer). This is a signature steamed rice cake. Because the white color represents purity and all things sacred, this rice cake has long been used for celebrations and traditional rituals. Koreans still make *baekseolgi* on the 100th-day celebrations of newborns or on first birthdays and share with friends and neighbors.

Ingredients for 25 cm in diameter steamer

2 1/2 cups of white rice | 1/2 Tbsp salt | 3/4 cup of sugar water | 1 Tbsp honey

> If the powder is pressed down in the steamer, the rice cake will become hard and uncooked, so make sure the powder is poured evenly without added pressure.
> You can add soaked black beans, raisins, chestnuts, or jujubes.
> Steam into flat thin disks to make rice cake sandwiches.

Tteok Culture

Tteok, or Korean rice cake, is made with steamed, boiled, or pan-fried flour made of various grains. There are over 200 varieties of *tteok* documented in historical records. Traditionally, it was an important dish that was always made for first birthdays, weddings, 60th birthdays, and a variety of rituals. People from all social class levels, from royalty and nobility to commoners, made *tteok* on special celebrations. It is still an important part of Korea cuisine.

Different types of *tteok*

183

1 Wash the rice thoroughly, soak for 3 to 4 hours, and drain. Add salt, blend into powder form, and sift the flour. (You can use your local mill.)

2 Boil 1 cup of water with 1/2 cup of sugar to make syrup and let it cool.

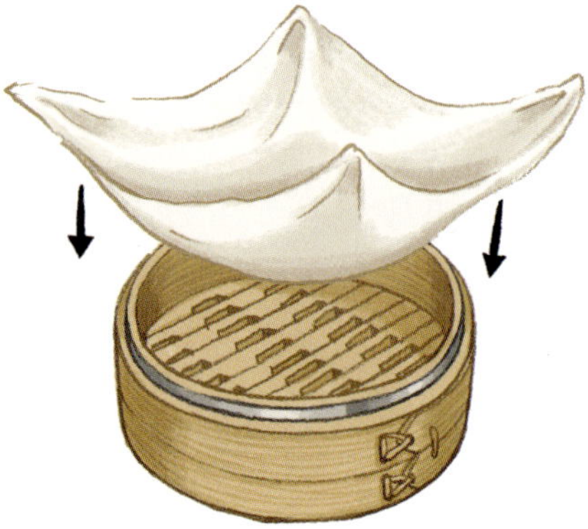

3 Add honey and syrup to the flour and mix the flour well with both hands. When it is moist sift the flour again.

4 Lay wet cotton cooking cloth on a bamboo steamer.

> *Tteok* was traditionally steamed in an earthenware steamer called *siru*. A *siru* is a round vessel with small holes in the bottom to let the steam in. The traditional *siru* is very heavy, so modern steamer is more widely used these days.

siru

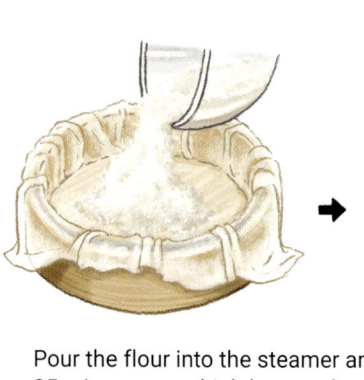

Pour the flour into the steamer and make the top flat. Steam for 25 minutes over high heat and another 5 minutes over low heat.

5 When the rice cake is cooked, remove the lid to cool and take out the rice cakes.

Place a tray over the rice cakes and flip it over.

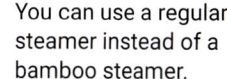

You can use a regular steamer instead of a bamboo steamer.

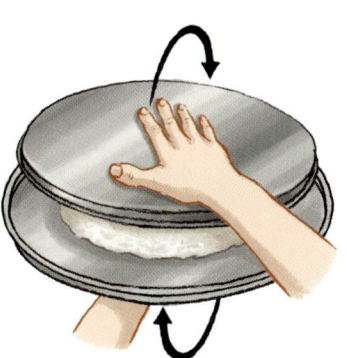

Remove the steamer and cotton cooking cloth.

Place another tray over the rice cakes and flip it over.

Cut into small pieces and serve.

Chapter 4
Dessert
&
Drink

화전
Hwajeon

Pan-fried Flower Rice Cake

Glutinous rice powder and boiling water are mixed together to make a dough. The dough is shaped into small round and flat pancakes decorated with dried jujube and crown daisies and pan-fried. Decorate with fresh seasonal flowers for a colorful variation.

Ingredients 12 pieces

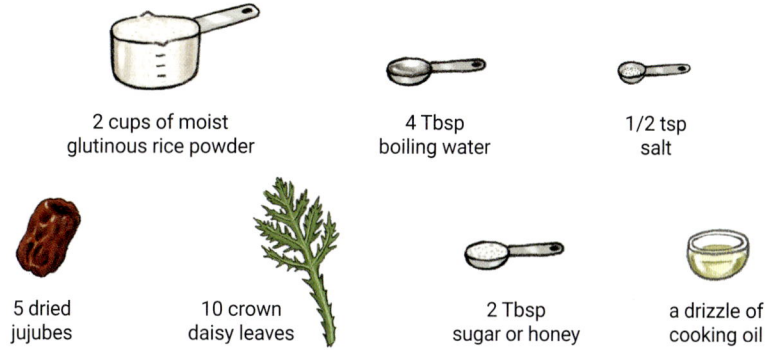

- 2 cups of moist glutinous rice powder
- 4 Tbsp boiling water
- 1/2 tsp salt
- 5 dried jujubes
- 10 crown daisy leaves
- 2 Tbsp sugar or honey
- a drizzle of cooking oil

When using dry glutinous rice powder :
2 cups of dry glutinous rice powder, 1/2 cup of water, 5 to 6 Tbsp of boiling water, 1/2 tsp salt

Hwajeon

Glutinous rice is made into a batter and pan-fried with oil. Fresh flowers are placed on top as decorations. Azalea, Cornelian cherry flower, and violet are used in the spring for *hwajeon*. Rose and cockscomb are used in the summer. Chrysanthemum is the flower of choice in the fall. Crown daisy leaves and dried jujubes can be used as decorations instead of flowers. It is a great way to enjoy different seasons.

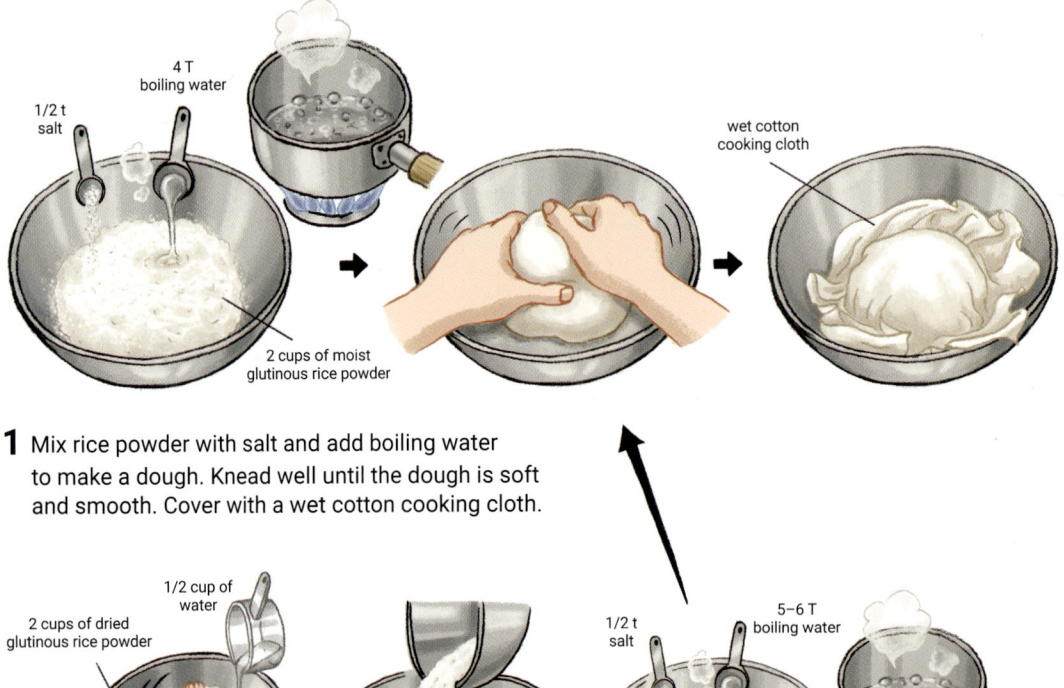

1 Mix rice powder with salt and add boiling water to make a dough. Knead well until the dough is soft and smooth. Cover with a wet cotton cooking cloth.

Rice cake, made with dry glutinous rice powder, can become hard when cooked, so add water to the rice powder to make it moist and sieve the powder before kneading it into a dough.

2 Cut the jujube around the pit, leaving a long piece of fruit. Flatten it out with a rolling pin. Tightly roll and slice to make small flowers.

Take the small leaves off of the crown daisy stem.

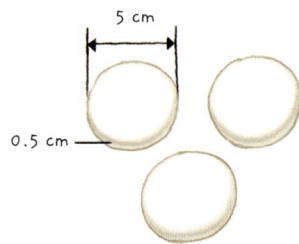

3 Make small pancakes from the dough 0.5 cm thick, 5 cm in diameter.

4 Pan-fry the rice cakes in a pan with oil without burning the bottom.

When the bottom is cooked and slightly translucent, flip it over and arrange the jujubes and crown daisy leaves.

Turn it over again and cook the other side briefly.

5 Sprinkle the sugar onto a tray.

Place the rice cakes on the tray and coat with sugar.

Serve on a plate. (Sprinkling on some cinnamon or pine nut powder is optional.)

Hwajeon-nori Culture

In the spring (the third day of the third month of the lunar calendar), the village people would go on picnics to nearby mountains and fields to enjoy the spring scenery and eat *hwajeon* or other types of rice cakes made with azaleas. This is called *hwajeon-nori* (*hwajeon* outings).

Chapter 4
Dessert
&
Drink

오미자화채
Omija-hwachae

Omija Punch

This Schisandra punch is made by infusing berries in water and adding Asian pear slices. The name of the punch differs depending on the fruit that is added to it. For example, one variation is called *bae-hwachae* (Asian pear punch).

Ingredients 4 servings

1/2 cup of dried Schisandra (*omija*)

5 cups of water

1 cup of sugar

1 1/2 cups of water

1/4 cup of honey

1/4 Asian pear

1 tsp pine nuts

small pinch of sugar

If you don't have Asian pear, you can add azaleas, cherries, peaches, or summer tangerines for a delicious variation.
Add sugar and honey according to taste.
The Schisandra can change the color of metallic materials, so use glass, plastics, or tin bowls for the infusion.

What is *omija*?

Omija or Schisandra is harvested in the fall and dried for storage to be used up until the following year. Dried berries are dark red in color and become sticky. It is best to keep the dried berries in the fridge for longer storage.

It is written in *Donguibogam* that "the skin and fruit of Schisandra are sweet and sour, the seeds are spicy and bitter, and yet they all have a salty flavor. That is why they are called *omija* (five-flavor berry), because they contain all the five flavors. Each flavor heals a different organ in the body: the sour for the liver, the spicy for the lungs, the bitter for the heart, the salty for the kidneys, and the sweet for the spleen."

omija

dried *omija*

1 Wash and drain the berries.

2 Boil 5 cups of water, turn off the heat, and cool down to 40°C. Add the berries and infuse for 12 hours (24 hours if using cold water). When the water turns red, sieve the water using cotton cooking cloth to remove the berries.

3 Boil 1 1/2 cups of water with 1 cup of sugar. Turn off the heat and add 1/4 cup of honey. Let it cool and mix with the berry-infused water.

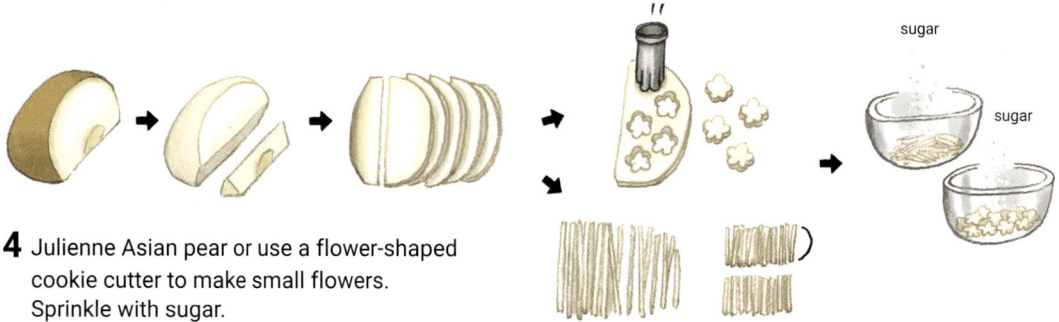

4 Julienne Asian pear or use a flower-shaped cookie cutter to make small flowers. Sprinkle with sugar.

5 Serve the punch in a bowl with pears and pine nuts.

What is *hwachae*?

Fruits or flower petals are added to *omija*-infused water sweetened with sugar or honey water. It is usually served cold and with pine nuts float.

Hwachae made with *omija*-infused water

Changmyeon **(Mung Bean Jelly Punch)**
Julienned mung bean jelly are added to *omija* water sweetened with honey.

Jindallae-hwachae **(Azalea Punch)**
Azalea is coated with starch, blanched, and cooled in cold water, and added to the surface of *omija* water.

Borisudan **(Barley Punch)**
Cooked barley is coated with starch, blanched, and added to *omija* water. (It can also be added to honey water.)

Hwachae made with honey water

Yuja-hwachae **(*Yuzu* Punch)**
Yuzu is pitted, cut into small pieces and sprinkled with sugar or honey. The outer and inner part of the *yuzu* skin are thinly sliced and arranged in a bowl with Asian pear slices and *yuzu* pieces. Honey water or sugar water is poured into the bowl and float pomegranate and pine nuts.

Wonsobyeong **(Sweet Rice Ball Punch)**
Small rice balls made with glutinous rice powder and each dyed in different colors are added to honey water.

Aengdu-hwachae **(Cherry Punch)**
Pitted cherries are soaked in honey and added to honey water and pine nuts float.

Chapter 4
Dessert
&
Drink

수정과
Sujeonggwa
Cinnamon Punch

Sujeonggwa, meaning "biscuit dipped in water," is a Korean traditional beverage enjoyed cold in the winter. Water, boiled with ginger and cinnamon, is boiled again with sugar and cooled and served with dried persimmon placed in the drink. The spicy flavor of ginger and cinnamon goes well with the sweetness of the dried persimmon.

Ingredients 4 servings

| 4 dried persimmons | 30 g ginger | 20 g cinnamon stick | 1 cup of brown sugar | 6 cups of water | 1 tsp pine nuts |

Sujeonggwa is served cold, but it can also be enjoyed hot.

Korean Traditional Beverage

From long ago, Koreans have been making various beverages using a wide range of ingredients, including medicinal herbs, berries, flower petals, tea leaves, and fruit. The ingredients were prepared in many different ways to make the drinks. Some of those ways are boiling them as a whole, soaking it in honey and mixing it with water, or drying it and infusing it like tea. Aside from *sujeonggwa*, other traditional drinks are *yuzu* tea, jujube tea, *sikhye* (rice beverage), *songhwamilsu* (pine pollen honey drink), and *misu* (multigrain drink).

Yujacha
(*Yuzu* Tea)

Daechucha
(Jujube Tea)

Sikhye
(Rice Beverage)

Cooked white rice is fermented in malt water.

Songhwamilsu
(Pine Pollen Honey Drink)

Pine pollen is mixed with honey water or sugar water.

Misu
(Multgrain Drink)

Rice and other grains are steamed, dried, and ground into powder form and mixed with honey water.

1 Peel the ginger and cut into thin slices. Cut the cinnamon stick into small pieces.

2 Boil the ginger and cinnamon in water. Turn down the heat to low when the water starts to boil and simmer for 30 minutes. Pour the liquid over a cotton cooking cloth to remove the solid ingredients.

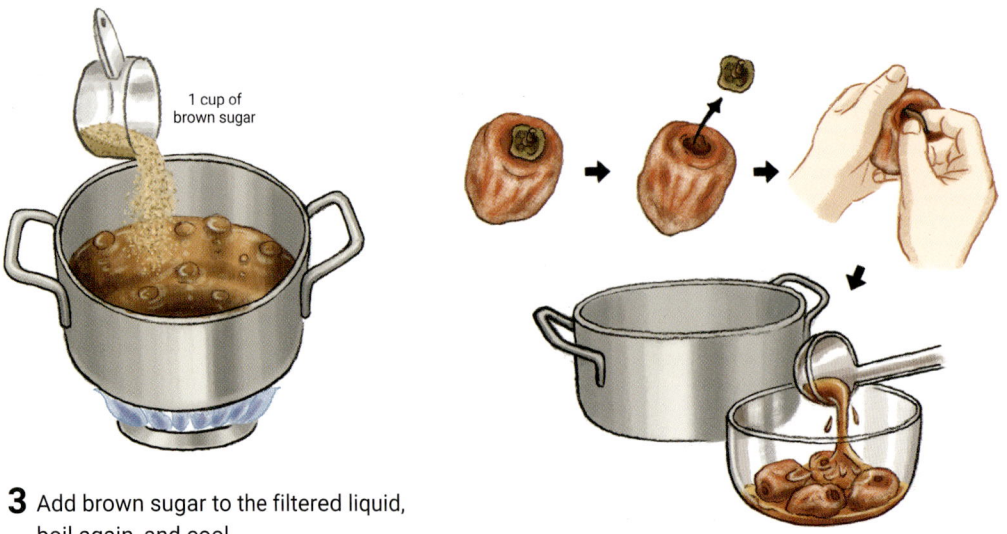

3 Add brown sugar to the filtered liquid, boil again, and cool.

4 Remove the stem and seeds from the dried persimmon and pour the cooled liquid over the fruits to soften them. (Adjust the duration of soaking depending on the softness of the fruits.)

5 Serve punch and dried persimmon in a bowl with pine nuts float. (You can leave out the dried persimmon if not available.)

Traditional Tea Tray

Dagwasang is the traditional tray or small table arranged with small confections and other traditional delicacies with tea or punch. It is prepared for guests and sometimes served after a meal as a dessert. This traditional tea served on elegant wooden tables is a unique table setting portraying the warm hospitality of Koreans. The desserts change according to the season, and usually, one drink is served with either a small delicacy or rice cake.

Spring
- azalea hwachae
- maejakgwa
- hwajeon

Summer
- jeonggwa
- jeungpyeon
- watermelon hwachae

Fall
- daechucho
- yullan
- baekseolgi
- baesuk

Winter
- gangjeong
- yakgwa
- sikhye

Index

A
Asian pear • 13, 192
Asian pear juice • 20, 84
aengdu-hwachae (cherry punch) • 193
aetang-guk (mugwort soup) • 10
anchovy, dried anchovies • 47, 69, 119

B
baechu-kimchi (kimchi) • 10, 134
baek-kimchi (white kimchi) • 141
baekseolgi (snow white rice cake) • 182
baesuk • 197
banchan • 72
Bansangcharim • 11
bap (rice) • 26
barley • 13, 15, 31, 193
bean sprouts *namul* (*kongnamul*) • 146–149
beef brisket • 13, 61
beef *jeon* (*yukwonjeon*) • 106–109
bellflower *root* • 13, 22, 35, 36
bibimbap • 34
bibim-guksu • 49
bibim-naengmyeon • 51
bindaetteok (mung bean pancake) • 110
binjatteok (*bingja*) • 111
birthday meal • 31, 65
borisudan (barley punch) • 193
bossam (napa wraps with pork) • 176
bossam-kimchi (wrapped kimchi) • 141
brown rice • 27
budae-jjigae • 77
bulgogi • 85, 127, 129
burdock • 39–41
bureom (various nuts) • 33

C
condiments • 14–17
chadolbagi doenjang-jjigae (beef brisket soybean paste stew) • 75
chalbap (rice made with glutinous rice and red bean) • 31, 65
chamchi (tuna) gimbap • 39
changmyeon (mung bean jelly punch) • 193
chard • 69
cheese gimbap • 39
cheonggukjang-jjigae (rich soybean paste stew) • 10
chonggak-kimchi (ponytail radish kimchi) • 139
chonggak-mu (ponytail radish) • 139
chungmu-gimbap • 39

cooking oil • 17
corn syrup • 17
croaker stew • 11
curled mallow • 69

D
daechucha (*jujube tea*) • 195
daechucho • 197
daepa (green onion) • 115
dakjuk (chicken porridge) • 173
dangmyeon (glass noodles) • 165
difference between steak and *neobiani* • 85
different types of *garaetteok* • 169
different types of green onions • 115
different types of kimchi • 141
different types of *mul*-kimchi • 143
different types of *oi*-kimchi • 131
different types of *tteok* • 183
doenjang (soybean paste) • 10, 15, 16, 68
doenjang-jjigae (soybean paste stew) • 71
dolsot-bibimbap (hot stone pot bibimbap) • 35
dongchimi (radish water kimchi) • 141, 143
dongtae-jjigae (pollack stew) • 75
Donguibogam • 12, 43, 65, 173, 191
dubugui (pan-fried bean curd) • 86
dubujorim (braised tofu) • 87
dureup-jeon (pan-fried fatsia sprout) • 10
dwaeji galbi-jjim (braised pork ribs) • 91

E
electric rice cooker • 28

F
fernbrake • 22, 36, 63
fernbrake *namul* • 36–37, 147
fish cake • 39–41, 119–121
fish *jeon* (*saengseonjeon*) • 106–109

G
galbi-jjim (braised short ribs) • 90
gangjeong • 197
garaetteok (cylinder-shaped white rice cake) • 169, 183
garnish • 18
gimbap • 38
ginger juice • 20
ginkgo nuts • 13, 18, 153, 156
glutinous millet • 13, 31
gochujang • 10, 16
gochutgaru • 16, 17
godeungeo-jorim (braised mackerel) • 98
godeungeo-gui (grilled mackerel) • 99
godeungeo-kimchi *jorim* (braised kimchi mackerel) • 99

ggoma (mini) gimbap • 39
green onions • 13, 17–19
grilled dried pollack • 11
groundsel • 177
gujeolpan (platter of nine delicacies) • 158
guk • 58
guksu-jangguk (noodles in hot beef-based broth) • 46
gukwha (chrysanthemum) *hwajeon* • 187
gungjung-tteokbokki (royal stir-fried rice cakes) • 168
gyuasang (cucumber dumplings) • 55

H

haemul-pajeon (seafood and green onion pancake) • 114
hamheung-naengmyeon • 51
hangari (clay pot) • 15, 141
history of *bindaetteok* • 111
history of *tteokbokki* • 119
hobakjuk (pumpkin porridge) • 42
hoe-bibimbap (raw fish bibimbap) • 35
hwachae (punch) • 193
hwajeon (pan-fried flower rice pancake) • 186
hwajeon-nori • 189
hwayangjeok • 107
hyeonmi-bap (brown rice) • 27

J

jangmi (rose) *hwajeon* • 187
japchae (stir-fried glass noodles and vegetables) • 164
jatjuk (pine nut porridge) • 42
jebiggot (violet) *hwajeon* • 187
jeok • 107
jeon • 107
jeonggwa • 197
jeongol (hot pot) • 153
Jeongwol Daeboreum • 33
jeungpyeon • 197
jeyuk-bokkeum (spicy stir-fried pork) • 122
jeyuk-deopbap • 125
jijimnureum-jeok • 107
jindallae (azalea) *hwajeon* • 187, 197
jindallae-hwachae (azalea punch) • 193
jidan • 18, 21
jip-ganjang • 14, 15
jjigae (stew) • 75
jjimdak (soy sauce-braised chicken) • 95
jjin mandu (steamed dumplings) • 55
jjokpa (small green onion) • 115
juksun malgeun-tang (bamboo shoot soup) • 61
julienne radish fresh salad (*musaengchae*) • 146–149, 179

K

kelp • 13, 18, 177
kidney beans • 31

kimchi and chilis in Korean food • 145
kimchi-*bokkeumbap* (kimchi fried rice) • 103
kimchi fermentation • 141
kimchi *jeyuk-bokkeum* • 125
kimchi-*jeok* (kimchi skewers) • 105
kimchi-*jeon* (kimchi pancake) • 102
kimchi-*jjigae* (kimchi stew) • 74
kimjang • 135
kkakdugi (diced radish kimchi) • 138
Korean chive fresh *namul* (*saengchae*) • 147
Korean zucchini *jeon* (*aehobakjeon*) • 106–109

L

lettuce • 13, 177, 179

M

maejakgwa • 197
maeun dak-jjim (spicy braised chicken) • 94
makgeolli • 113
making *sari* (noodle mound) • 53
making toasted sesame seeds • 22
making tofu • 89
mandut-guk (dumpling soup) • 54
manna lichen mushrooms • 18, 153, 155
meju • 14, 15
minarichodae (pan-fried water parsley) • 18, 93, 155
mincing garlic • 19
mincing ginger • 19
mincing green onion • 19
misu (multigrain drink) • 195
miyeongnaeng-guk (chilled seaweed soup) • 67
miyeok (seaweed) • 65
miyeok-guk (seaweed soup) • 31, 64, 65
mu (daikon radish) • 13, 61, 139
mubineul-kimchi (daikon radish kimchi stuffed with spicy seasonings) • 139
mul-kimchi (water kimchi) • 143
mul-naengmyeon (cold buckwheat noodles) • 50
mung bean • 13, 111
mung bean sprouts • 111
mung bean sprouts *namul* • 147
modum-jeon (assorted savory pancakes) • 106
mustard • 17
mustard sauce • 53, 162
myeolchi (anchovy) • 69
myeolchiaekjeot (anchovy sauce) • 17

N

nabak-kimchi (spicy water kimchi) • 142
namul (seasoned vegetables) • 146, 147
neobiani (marinated grilled beef slices) • 10, 82
nooroongji • 29, 97
nuts • 13, 33

O

ogokbap (steamed five-grain rice) • 30, 33
oi-gamjeong (cucumber stew) • 75, 133
oi-jangajji (cucumber pickle) • 10
oi-kimchi (cucumber kimchi) • 130
oi-namul (seasoned cucumber) • 133
oi-saengchae (cucumber salad) • 133
oi-seon (stuffed cucumber) • 133
oi-sobagi (stuffed cucumber kimchi) • 131
oi-songsongi/oi-kkakdugi (diced cucumber kimchi) • 131
omasum • 153, 156
omija (Schisandra) • 191
omija-hwachae (omija punch) • 190
osam-bulgogi • 125

P

pa-kimchi (green onion kimchi) • 141
paganghoe (blanched green onion wrap) • 115
perilla leaves • 13, 177, 179
pimpinella *namul* • 147
pine nut • 13, 43
pine nut powder • 22
pojangmacha (street vendors) • 121
pumpkin leaves • 177
pyeonsu (zucchini dumplings) • 55

R

rehydrating dried fernbrake • 22

S

saeng-chaeso bibimbap (fresh vegetable bibimbap) • 35
saeujeot (salted shrimp) • 10, 17, 131
samgyeopsal-gui (grilled pork belly) • 179
samgyetang (ginseng chicken soup) • 10, 172
samsaek-namul (three seasoned vegetables) • 146
seasoned dried vegetables • 33
seaweed • 65
sigeumchi doenjang-guk (spinach soybean paste soup) • 68
sikhye (rice beverage) • 195, 197
silpa (thread green onion) • 115
sinseollo (royal hot pot) • 152
siru (traditional steamer) • 184
softening mung bean jelly • 20
sogogi (beef) gimbap • 39
sogogimut-guk (beef and radish soup) • 60
songhwamilsu (pine pollen honey drink) • 195
songpyeon (half-moon rice cake) • 10, 183
soongnyung • 29
soybeans • 13, 31
soy-vinegar dipping sauce • 57, 105, 109, 113, 117, 162
spinach *namul* (*sigeumchinamul*) • 146–149
ssam • 177
ssamjang • 16, 177

steamer • 185
stir-fried chilis and anchovies • 11
sujeonggwa (cinnamon punch) • 194
sundae • 121
sundubu-jjigae (soft bean curd stew) • 78
sweet pickled *radish* • 39
sweet potato stem *namul* • 147

T

taro stem • 22, 63
taro stem *namul* • 147
toasted laver • 11, 33, 39, 41
tofu • 79, 81
tofu stew • 11
toran-tang (taro soup) • 10, 61
traditional tea tray • 197
tteok (rice cake) culture • 183
tteokbokki (spicy stir-fried rice cakes) • 118
tteokbokki cooked on the table • 119
tteokguk (rice cake soup) • 169
tteok-sanjeok • 107
ttukbaegi-bulgogi (hot pot bulgogi) • 126
twigim • 121

V

vinegar • 17
violet *hwajeon* • 187

W

white rice • 13, 27, 31
walnut • 13, 18, 156
watermelon *hwachae* • 197
winter cabbage • 69
wonsobyeong (sweet rice ball punch) • 193

Y

yangjo-ganjang • 15
yakgwa • 197
Yaksikdongwon • 12
Yin-Yang Five Elements • 12
yujacha (yuzu tea) • 195
yuja-hwachae (yuzu punch) • 193
yukgaejang (spicy beef soup) • 63
yuk-hoe bibimbap (raw beef bibimbap) • 35
yullan • 197